THINK
PARENTING
Bloom

Heather Vardon

contents

part one
parenting approaches and communication

part two
children's emotional well-being

part three
family dynamics and relationships

part four
part iv: closing

The information contained in this book is based upon the research and personal experiences of the author. It is not intended as a substitute for consulting with your physician or other healthcare provider. Any attempt to diagnose and treat an illness, should only be done under the direction of a healthcare professional.

The publisher does not advocate the use of any particular healthcare protocol, but believes the information in this book should be available to the public. The publisher and author are not responsible for any adverse effects or consequences, resulting from the use of the ideas or activities discussed in this book. Should the reader have any questions, the author and the publisher strongly suggest consulting a professional healthcare advisor.

To the child I once was ~ outspoken, sensitive, searching for love and truth in a home where words often went unspoken.

To the parents who did their best, even when silence filled the space where connection could have lived.

To my own children ~ thank you for teaching me to slow down, lean in, and listen with both ears and heart.

To every parent trying to unlearn patterns and create new ones,

To every child still hoping to be seen, heard, and accepted ~ this book is for all of us.

For the generations before us, the ones we are raising now, and the hope that we can rewrite the story ~ with honesty, love, and connection leading the way.

I know what it feels like to love deeply but not know how to show it.

To want to be seen and not know how to speak.

To parent while still healing the child inside of me.

This book was born from that journey ~ the messy, beautiful, everyday work of learning love in real time.

May we remember this: the most meaningful moments are often the messy ones ~ the ones we try to fix, shape, or rush through.

Even in frustration, even in the chaos, these moments are sacred. We are more blessed than we know.

Even in the times when it feels hard to love, we often look back and see that love was always there ~ or that it could have made all the difference.

So here's to love ~ even when it's hard, even when we're just surviving.

We won't always get it right, but love gives us a place to begin again.

May this book be a small reminder: love makes it lighter.

Love to all.

personal message from the author

Note on the Cover:

The cover of this book was created with intention. The parents are dressed in athletic gear, ready for a nature walk, while their child wears a skirt, not typical "athletic" clothing. This choice was purposeful ~ it represents allowing children to show up as themselves, to express their individuality, and to make choices without worrying about fitting expectations. The child stands out, celebrated for being herself, just as we hope every child's authentic self will be honored and nurtured throughout this book.

The Heart of This Book

The purpose of this book is to support all children and parents ~ which ultimately means everyone ~ because, as adults, we are all just grown-up children. Many of us carry unresolved wounds from childhood into adulthood, shaping how we see ourselves, how we connect with others, and how we parent. The world can be cruel, and its pressures, judgments, and traumas often leave marks that we may not even recognize. We are not alone in this experience; together, we can learn to face these truths with compassion, awareness, and courage.

I am not a professional, doctor, or psychologist. I have walked my own difficult path, including extensive therapy, confronting addiction, and facing challenges that forced me to meet my own pain head-on. Over time, I began to uncover my true self and separate my authentic identity from the programmed beliefs I absorbed in childhood.

That journey of self-discovery has taught me the importance of reflection, self-awareness, and living in alignment with my heart and values. It is how I found who I truly am, and it is from this place of honesty and vulnerability that this book is written.

Everything in this book stems from my personal journey ~ as a child, a teenager, an adult, and a parent. Along the way, I have gained insight not only into myself but also into the intricate world of parenting. Raising my own children has been one of my greatest teachers. I have learned from their reactions to my choices, from my mistakes, and from reflecting on what I could have done differently. Parenting has forced me to confront my patterns, my blind spots, and my inherited ways of thinking, and in doing so, it has offered profound opportunities for growth and healing.

As a parent, I have also witnessed countless interactions between other parents and their children. I have seen how these relationships are shaped by both nurturing and damaging patterns, often carried from the parent's own unhealed trauma. These experiences have taught me just how deeply past pain can affect our self-image and parenting style, often without our conscious awareness. I have seen the heartbreak of misunderstandings, the long shadows of unresolved wounds, and the beauty that comes when parents choose to engage with love, awareness, and presence.

The goal of this book is to help readers recognize how profoundly our actions, words, and behaviors shape our children's lives. We hold the power to build them up ~ or, without meaning to, to break them down. We can be the reason they thrive, or the reason they struggle. That is why it is so important to reflect on our own childhoods: to understand how those early experiences continue to shape us, not only as individuals but also as parents. By facing our own pain, observing our patterns, and choosing intentional, mindful ways of responding, we can break generational cycles and create a new path for our children ~ one rooted in love, compassion, and authenticity.

It took me a year to write this book, and every word comes from my heart, soul, and lived experiences ~ my mistakes, failures, accomplishments, periods of growth, stagnant moments, sorrow, joy, and frustration. This journey reflects my path of finding myself and facing the internal wounds carried from childhood, school, home, and society. Everything shared here comes from my own life and discoveries ~ there is no finger pointing, not even at my parents. My intention is love: to offer guidance and support for parents and individuals seeking to find happiness within themselves and, in turn, nurture it in their children.

I recognize that our world can be a difficult and challenging place. Even with the best intentions at home, outside traumas ~ school, community, society ~ can still leave scars. No parent can shield a child from all pain, and yet, we can create a strong, loving foundation ~ a pillar of guidance ~ that equips them to face life with confidence and authenticity. My hope is that this book provides that foundation: a safe, intentional, and conscious approach to raising children so they can grow into their true selves, feel seen, and embrace their own identity without needing to seek validation through outside accomplishments or external approval.

Parenting is sacred, sometimes messy, and always a transformative journey. It asks us to look inward, to recognize our own wounds, and to remain present with both our children and ourselves. It is through this commitment to awareness, reflection, and love that we can create spaces of growth, healing, and authenticity.

I see every parent and child who reads this, and I accept and honor each of you. You are not alone. Together, we can navigate the challenges, the heartbreak, and the beauty of this world. This work is about love, awareness, and creating space for growth, healing, and the freedom to be fully oneself. It is my hope that this book serves as a companion, a guide, and a reminder that while the world may be harsh at times, we can face it with courage, heart, and connection ~ together.

Children enter this world as pure, innocent beings, untouched by the complexities and hardships that life will eventually present. They are like blank canvases, full of potential and wonder, eager to absorb the love, wisdom, and guidance of those entrusted with their care. As parents, it is our sacred responsibility to be their angels ~ to nurture, guide, and protect them with unwavering devotion. We hold the power to shape their hearts and minds, to teach them values, to offer comfort, and to shield them from harm while encouraging their growth. In doing so, we help them move through the world with confidence and compassion, allowing them to blossom into kind, grounded individuals ~ strong in character, secure in self-worth, and unafraid to live as their most authentic selves, no matter what the world expects of them.

To become the best parents we can be, we must first pause and take an honest look in the mirror. Self-awareness is essential ~ it allows us to recognize our faults, acknowledge our wounds, and prevent our struggles from being unknowingly passed down to our children. For me, parenthood brought many of my own childhood traumas to the surface ~ some of which I now realize were passed down across generations. I made the conscious decision to parent differently, to break that cycle. My parents did the best they could with what they knew, but some of the methods passed down through generations left unseen wounds ~ more silence than connection. I've come to understand that they were carrying their own unhealed stories, and their way of loving was shaped by what they had learned. Still, I knew I wanted to break that quiet inheritance ~ to offer my children what I once needed myself. I wanted to raise them in light, not in the fog of confusion or the shadows of what was never spoken. My hope has always been to parent with awareness, compassion, and healing at the center, so my children can grow up feeling seen, safe, and free to be who they truly are.

So far, this shift ~ built in awareness, compassion, and a commitment to breaking old patterns ~ has made all the difference. By approaching parenting with intention, understanding, and a focus on nurturing my children's authentic selves, I've seen how love, guidance, and empathy can transform not only their lives but my own. My children have not faced the same emotional burdens I carried, and for that, I am endlessly grateful. My hope in sharing this is simple: if these words can help even one person begin to heal from childhood trauma or prevent a child from carrying unnecessary pain into adulthood, then I will have fulfilled my purpose.

Let us raise our children with love as our foundation. With compassionate eyes that see without judgment, hearts open without expectation, and ears that listen without interruption, may we guide them to grow into their fullest, most authentic selves ~ their own star, their own snowflake.

May they walk their true path, fulfill their heart's deepest desires, and enrich not only their own lives but also the lives of those they touch along the way.

A Letter From Heather

Dear Parent,

Thank you for picking up this book and for showing up with an open heart. Choosing to read, to reflect, and to pay attention to your child ~ and to yourself ~ is a powerful act. Parenting is not about perfection. It is about presence, curiosity, and the willingness to keep learning, even when it feels hard.

This book grew beyond anything I expected. There was so much important material I wanted to share that it became necessary to divide it into two parts. You now hold the first part, *Bloom*, and it is filled with ideas, reflections, and tools to help you notice, understand, and connect with your child in ways you may not have before. Every chapter, every insight, every pause is a seed planted in the soil of your parenting journey.

Small moments of awareness can grow into lasting change. Each choice you make to slow down, reflect, and respond with thoughtfulness helps you break cycles, heal old patterns, and create a safer, more loving environment for your child. Your willingness to engage in this work matters more than you know.

As you read, I hope you feel both challenged and supported. I hope you discover truths that empower you, and insights that guide you. Most of all, I hope you see that the love you pour into this work has the power to ripple through your child, your family, and generations to come.

This is only the beginning. The seeds planted in *Bloom* are ready to grow. When you're ready, the next book, *Flourish*, will guide you in tending those seeds, helping them take root, and turning awareness into action, reflection into habit, and insight into lasting connection.

Keep noticing.
Keep reflecting.
Keep planting seeds.
Keep choosing love.

Thank you for trusting yourself and for choosing to grow alongside your child. This journey is not easy, yet every step you take is meaningful, and you are not walking it alone.

With all my love and gratitude,

Heather

Stop and Think

Words cannot be undone. Even a single word, like "disappointed," can leave a mark on a child's heart that lingers far longer than we realize.

As parents, we set an example. That's why it's so important to pause and think before we act or speak in ways that might cause our children to lose respect for us, to see us in a negative light, to stop trusting us, to not want to be like us, or even to distance themselves from our lives. The way we show up for them today shapes how they see themselves, us, and the world around them.

Let's aim to parent with both our hearts and minds ~ raising children who are balanced, confident, and emotionally healthy. Of course, no one is perfect. We all make mistakes, but each one offers an opportunity to grow, to repair, and to love more consciously.

Mistakes will happen, but what matters most is that we remain aware ~ that we stay open, listen deeply, and take time to reflect on how our words and actions truly affect our children.

When we parent with intention, we begin to grow into the best version of ourselves. In doing so, we create the space for our children to become the best version of themselves, too.

Parenting is a lifelong journey. While perfection may be out of reach, mindfulness is not. The more aware we are of our influence, the stronger and healthier our connection with our children will become ~ and that's a gift that benefits us all!

Think...

It's important to pause and check in with ourselves. Are we feeling emotionally overwhelmed or mentally drained? Are there unresolved struggles we've been carrying that need attention? If so, seeking support isn't a sign of weakness ~ it's a necessary step toward becoming the parent our children truly need.

This book isn't just about helping children ~ it's just as much about helping parents grow, heal, and evolve alongside them. As you move through these pages, you might find reflections of your own childhood or notice triggers that surface during your parenting journey. These moments are powerful opportunities for awareness and change.

When we recognize and face these emotional patterns, we open the door to healing ~ not just for ourselves but for our families. The more we grow in self-understanding, the more we can guide our children with empathy, strength, and authenticity. This journey isn't one-sided. It's not just about their transformation. It's about yours, too.

Childhood Trauma Can Be Manifested in Many Ways into Adulthood

Childhood Trauma and Its Lasting Effects

Childhood trauma can show up in many ways throughout adulthood ~ mentally, emotionally, physically, and even in the way we parent.

The purpose of this book is to help us stay ahead of these patterns ~ to raise emotionally healthy, confident children through intentional parenting built on love, empathy, and understanding. As we learn and grow through the insights in these pages, we begin to guide our children ~ and ourselves ~ with greater awareness and compassion. Along the way, we start to recognize where our own wounds, insecurities, or unhealed experiences may surface, so we don't unintentionally pass them on or project them onto the ones we love most. Through this shared learning and healing, we create space for growth, connection, and lasting change ~ breaking old cycles and building a foundation of love that can carry through generations.

How We Can Prevent Childhood Trauma

1. Build a Safe and Supportive Environment

- **Physical Safety:** Create a home where your child feels protected from harm, chaos, and conflict.
- **Emotional Safety:** Make your home a judgment-free space where feelings can be expressed without fear or shame.

2. Prioritize Open Communication

- **Listen Fully:** Give your child your full attention. Validate what they feel ~ even when you don't fully understand it.
- **Encourage Expression:** Teach your child that all feelings are welcome, and it's okay to ask for help or clarity.

3. Practice Emotional Awareness and Regulation

- **Show What It Looks Like:** Let your child see how you handle emotions with care ~ taking a breath, stepping away when needed, or finding calm before responding.
- **Be Open About Your Feelings:** Share your own experiences in age-appropriate ways so your child understands that all emotions are part of being human.
- **Guide Them Through Big Feelings:** Help your child name what they're feeling and find healthy ways to express it ~ through words, movement, art, or reflection.
- **Teach Helpful Tools:** Practice simple strategies together like deep breathing, journaling, or talking with someone they trust.
- **Grow Together:** As you both learn to pause, reflect, and respond with understanding, you build a shared emotional language rooted in love and awareness.

4. Nurture Self-Worth

- **Celebrate Uniqueness:** Remind your child that who they are is enough ~ no achievements required.
- **Use Positive Reinforcement:** Praise effort and growth over perfection. Avoid comparisons to others.

5. Set Healthy Boundaries

- **Consistency Builds Trust:** Set clear, age-appropriate limits and follow through with love and respect.
- **Guide with Compassion:** Discipline is about teaching, not shame. Approach correction with understanding, avoiding fear.

6. Be Present and Engaged

- **Quality Over Quantity:** Spend intentional time together doing what your child enjoys.
- **Show Interest:** Be curious about their world ~ their friends, feelings, and dreams.

7. Heal Your Own Wounds

- **Reflect Often:** Notice how your past experiences shape the way you parent today.
- **Seek Support:** Healing your own trauma allows you to parent from awareness and peace. Therapy, mindfulness, reading, journaling, and open conversations can all be powerful tools for growth.

8. Provide Resources and Support

- **Mental Health Care:** If your child shows signs of distress, don't hesitate to seek guidance from a professional or trusted mentor.
- **Keep Learning:** Explore parenting books, podcasts, workshops, and communities that nurture understanding, reflection, and growth.

9. Encourage Independence

- **Let Them Explore:** Give your child space to make mistakes and learn from them.
- **Empower Decisions:** Involve them in choices that build confidence and trust in themselves.

10. Love Without Conditions

- **Show Affection Daily:** Express love through hugs, kind words, and your presence.
- **Accept Fully:** Let your child know they are loved for who they are ~ always.

How Childhood Trauma Can Manifest in Adulthood

Even when we can't always see it, trauma from childhood can live quietly within us.

Here are some of the most common ways it can show up:

Emotional Signs

- Anxiety, fear, or feeling unsafe even in calm situations.
- Persistent sadness or loss of joy.
- Intense emotions or mood swings that feel hard to manage.
- Low self-worth or difficulty accepting praise.

Behavioral Signs

- Struggles with trust or fear of abandonment.
- Unhealthy relationship patterns or codependency.
- Perfectionism or the need to overachieve.
- Addictive behaviors ~ food, substances, or habits used to cope.
- Avoiding reminders of pain or discomfort.

Physical Signs

- Chronic pain, fatigue, or frequent illness without clear cause.
- Sleep challenges ~ trouble falling asleep, staying asleep, or nightmares.

Cognitive Signs

- Difficulty concentrating or remembering.
- Racing thoughts or replaying painful memories.
- Constant feeling of being "on alert."

Social Signs

- Pulling away from others or feeling disconnected.

- Struggling to set or maintain healthy boundaries.

The Hope Beyond Trauma

When we choose awareness, healing, and compassion, we break cycles ~ not only for ourselves, but for our children.

Every step toward emotional safety, presence, and love creates the foundation for future generations to thrive.

Each day is a chance to connect, understand, and support your child's heart.

PART I:

PARENTING APPROACHES AND COMMUNICATION

"Welcome. Let's start this journey together. As we plant, water, and care, we grow alongside our children, discovering the beauty of every unfolding bloom. I'm here with you."
~ Heather

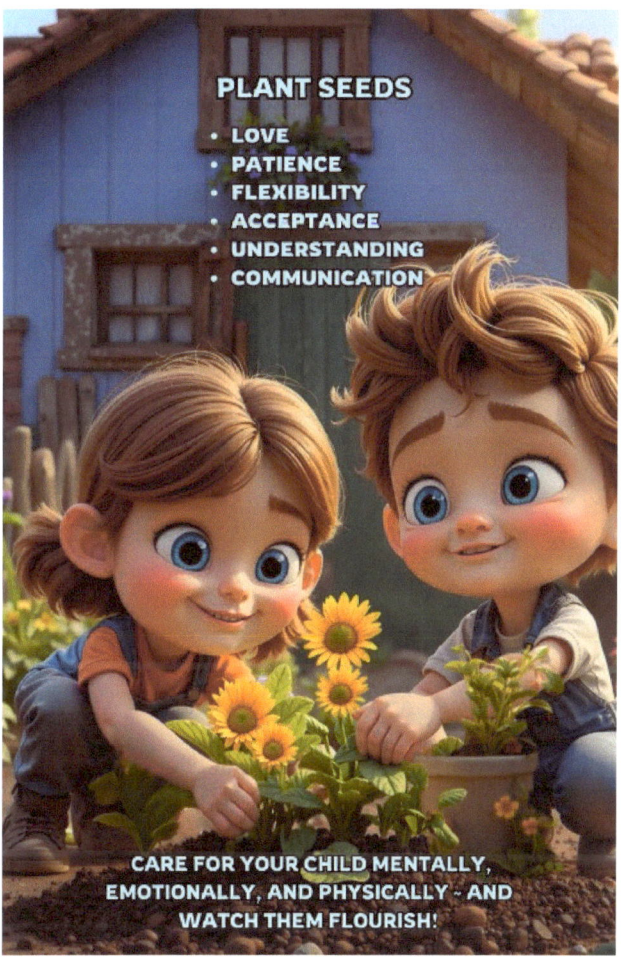

PLANT SEEDS

Planting the Seeds We Needed

Every child grows in the soil of the home they are raised in. The environment becomes the garden, and the adults become the gardeners. Children thrive when certain seeds are planted early ~ seeds of love, communication, patience, acceptance, and understanding. These seeds form the roots that help children feel safe enough to explore who they are and strong enough to express what they feel.

Take a moment to look back at your own childhood. Which seeds were plentiful in your garden? Which were sparse, or missing entirely? Some of us received love freely but lacked guidance. Others were nurtured with patience but struggled to hear words of encouragement. Some of us grew up filtering our needs, giving attention and care to siblings or others while our own roots went thirsty.

Remembering your childhood can bring a rush of feelings. You might notice moments when support was absent, when understanding or patience didn't come when it was needed most. You might feel guilt for wanting something more, anger for what was missing, or sadness at the quiet moments when your inner voice felt small. These reflections do not mean your parents failed; they simply show the humanity in every family and the limits of what was possible at that time.

Now, imagine your adult self standing in that childhood garden. How would you care for the younger version of you? Which seeds would you water more generously? Which moments of attention, patience, or understanding would you offer if you could? Recognizing these gaps is not about blame ~ it is about awareness, about under-standing what nourished you and what might have been missing. Awareness becomes fertile ground for change.

As a parent or caregiver today, you have the chance to give yourself the nourishment you once needed while also tending to your child. Some days you may need more water ~ more patience with yourself, more quiet moments, more recognition that growth is uneven and unique. Your child may need more sunlight or attention at times, and each stage teaches something important. Paying close attention, adjusting thoughtfully, and responding with care is how strong roots and healthy growth take hold.

Planting seeds is not a one-time act. Every hug, every listening ear, every patient pause is a drop of water, a shaft of sunlight, a gentle wind that helps your children ~ and you ~ grow. The choices you make today ripple into the future, creating a legacy of emotional strength, confi-dence, and freedom for generations to come.

Planting Seeds for Their Growth

Children grow best in an environment where love is steady and communication feels safe. Growth becomes possible when a child knows they can express emotions without fear, explore without judgment, and make mistakes without losing connection. These moments become the daily seeds that shape their inner world.

Healthy seeds look like patience during frustration, curiosity during conflict, and acceptance during big feelings. They look like slowing down long enough to listen, guiding without controlling, and showing understanding when emotions feel overwhelming. Children do not need perfection. They need presence, honesty, and a parent willing to see who they are becoming.

Every seed planted now becomes part of their story. Small moments accumulate into lifelong beliefs about themselves and the world. A child who is met with compassion learns to offer compassion. A child who receives understanding learns to trust their voice. A child who grows in the warmth of emotional safety learns to stand confidently in who they are.

Parenting with awareness allows you to plant the seeds you once needed. Parenting with intention allows you to offer your children nourishment that strengthens their roots. Planting these seeds creates a legacy of emotional wellness that reaches far beyond this moment.

The past may not have offered all the nourishment you needed, yet the present gives you the chance to plant what was missing. Every act of patience, every honest conversation, every moment of understanding becomes a seed that shapes a new story.

Plant the seeds you needed.

Plant the seeds your children need.

Plant the seeds that help them flourish in ways that heal generations.

Awareness becomes most powerful when it moves into action. The insights you've gained ~ noticing your own childhood needs, recognizing your emotions, and understanding how growth happens ~ can guide the way you show up for your children each day. Small, intentional acts become the sunlight, water, and soil that help their unique garden flourish. You don't need grand gestures or perfect parenting. Even simple, focused practices ~ one quality at a time ~ can plant meaningful seeds of connection, trust, and love that grow over time.

Activities:

These activities help you put your reflections into action and bring more care, attention, and connection into your everyday moments with your child.

1. Parent Reflection

- Which seeds did I need most as a child? How did I experience their absence or presence?
- How do the seeds I received influence the way I parent today?
- What seeds do I want to plant in my children? Which ones feel most urgent?
- What small actions or words can I use today to nurture growth in my children?
- How can I nurture myself so that I am a fertile ground for planting seeds?

2. A Week of Seeds

Choose one ~ communication, love, acceptance, patience, understanding, or flexibility ~ and make it your focus for the day. Tell your child what you're practicing and invite them to notice it with you.

🌱 Day One: Communication

Say, "Today I'm practicing communication." Try to really listen, without interrupting or jumping to fix. Speak your feelings clearly and calmly, and encourage your child to do the same.

🌱 Day Two: Love

Be generous with affection. Leave a note in their lunchbox, share a hug for no reason, or tell them, "I love you just for being you."

🌱 Day Three: Acceptance

Let things be as they are - messy room, big feelings, different opinions. Show them that love doesn't depend on perfection.

🌱 Day Four: Patience

Take a deep breath before responding. Give them space to explain or try again, reminding them that growth takes time.

🌱 Day Five: Understanding

Ask questions that help you see their world. "What made you feel that way?" "What do you need right now?" Listen like it's the most important thing you'll do all day.

🌱 Day Six: Flexibility

Let go of a plan. Say yes to playtime instead of chores. Show them that change can be met with calm and grace.

🌱 Day Seven: Presence

Take time to simply be with your child, fully and without distraction. Put away phones, screens, and to-do lists. Notice their expressions, listen to their stories, laugh together, and allow the moment to be exactly as it is. Presence shows your child that they matter deeply - not for what they do, but for who they are.

. . .

Remember: This isn't just about helping your child grow ~ it's about growing with them. Each day we practice, we plant a new seed of connection. Over time, those seeds become the roots of trust, strength, and love that will guide them long after they've grown.

WHAT IS LOVE?

Take a quiet moment and notice how love feels for you. Is it a hug, a kind word, time spent together, a thoughtful gesture, or someone seeing what you need without being asked? What makes your heart feel full, safe, or happy? There's no right or wrong answer ~ just notice what lights up your own heart.

As parents, one of the most important gifts we can give our children is helping them understand what love truly is and how it feels. We can guide them to recognize love that is nurturing, steady, and safe ~ love that makes them feel seen, valued, and secure. At the same time, we can help them understand that love is experienced and expressed in many different ways. Some people feel it in words, others in touch, in shared time, or in thoughtful actions. Helping them notice these differences allows them to understand their own hearts and recognize the many ways love shows up in the world. This awareness gives them a foundation for healthy relationships and a sense of belonging, teaching them that they are worthy of love just as they are.

The first step is to help your child experience love in ways they can feel and recognize. Show them what it looks and feels like through your words, gestures, attention, and presence. Describe it as a warm, light, butterfly-like feeling in their chest that brings a smile, lifts their mood, and makes them feel safe and happy. Invite them to notice it with you, to feel it in their body and heart. Through these shared moments, your child learns that love is never heavy, anxious, or confusing. They come to understand that love is gentle, steady, playful, and full of peace, joy, and belonging.

Paying attention to these small, heart-filled moments invites your child to experience love fully and to recognize it within themselves. These moments become a bridge between your heart and theirs, showing them that love is alive, present, and something they can feel, share, and carry with them.

As you move through the day, notice what makes your child's heart feel full. Watching them respond to a hug, a kind word, a shared laugh, or a thoughtful gesture gives you insight into how they experience love. Sometimes, the way you express love may not match the way your child feels it. Your awareness and presence allow you to meet their needs while showing them how to understand yours.

Exploring love together doesn't need to be complicated. It starts with noticing, sharing, and describing what fills the heart. When children learn what love feels like, they carry with them a sense of self-worth, empathy, and confidence in their relationships ~ the kind of foundation that supports them through challenges, hurts, and misunderstandings.

When we pay attention and describe what love feels like, we turn it from an idea into a living experience. We can help our children notice how it moves in their body, how it brightens their heart, and how it connects them to the people they care about. This awareness becomes a practice of shared presence, curiosity, and reflection ~ a way to teach love by showing it, naming it, and experiencing it together.

These reflections naturally lead into simple, heart-centered ways to explore love with your child. By noticing, sharing, and naming what makes your hearts feel full, you turn understanding into something your child can feel and carry with them every day.

Activities:

Here are some simple ways to explore love together, turning understanding into something you can feel and share.

How Love Feels

1. Notice what makes love feel real ~ for them and for you.

Take a moment to think about what makes your child feel most loved. Is it a hug? A small gift? Going to the park together? Being listened to? Something made just for them? These details matter because they tell you how your child experiences the world emotionally. At the same time, ask yourself what makes *you* feel loved. Thinking about your own heart opens the door for understanding each other in a deeper, more meaningful way.

The way we show love might not always match the way our children feel it. You might believe that spending time together is the most loving gesture, while your child might feel it through words of affirmation, a gentle touch, or an unexpected act of thoughtfulness. None of it is wrong; it's just different. Paying attention to how they receive love helps you meet their needs while also showing them how to understand yours.

When children learn what love feels like, they start building emotional strength. They carry with them a sense of self-worth, empathy, and confidence in their relationships - the kind of foundation that supports them through challenges, hurts, and misunderstandings.

2. Help them feel it for themselves.

Try a simple visualization exercise. Ask your child to close their eyes and picture different ways of feeling loved: being hugged, receiving a gift, spending time together, hearing "I love you," or getting help with something. After each one, pause and ask them to notice what they feel in their chest or heart.

Ask, "Which one made you feel the happiest, warmest, lightest inside?" That feeling is likely the way they most naturally receive love. Encourage them to put it into words if they can - maybe it feels like warmth, safety, joy, or comfort. This simple practice teaches them to recognize and name their feelings, which is the first step toward understanding themselves and others.

3. Notice the differences.

The way we show love might not always match the way our children feel it. You might believe that spending time together is the most loving gesture, while your child might feel it through words of affirmation, a gentle touch, or an unexpected act of thoughtfulness. None of it is wrong; it's just different. Paying attention to how they receive love helps you meet their needs while also showing them how to understand yours.

These activities are not about doing anything perfectly or finding a "right answer." They are meant to help you and your child notice and explore how love feels in real, everyday moments. By practicing these simple exercises ~ paying attention to hugs, kind words, shared laughs, or thoughtful gestures ~ you are helping your child recognize the ways they feel loved and learn how to express it themselves. At the same time, you deepen your own understanding of your heart and your patterns of giving and receiving love. Doing this together builds connection, trust, and empathy. Over time, these small, intentional moments add up, teaching your child that they are seen, understood, and always worthy of love, while also strengthening the bond you share.

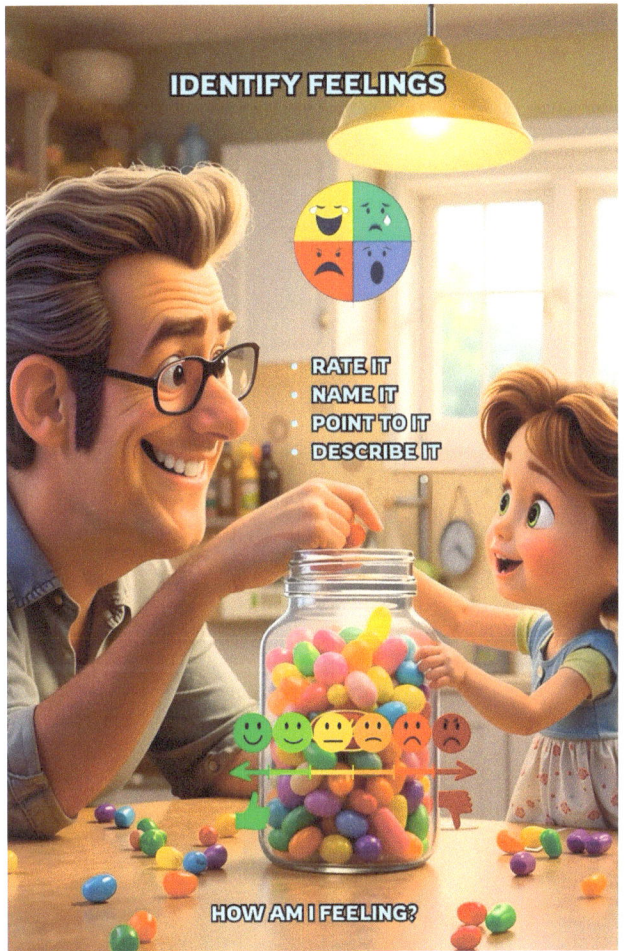

IDENTIFY FEELINGS

One of the most meaningful lessons we can offer our children is how to recognize and name their feelings. Emotional awareness doesn't always come naturally, especially for young children who are just beginning to understand the world around them and don't yet have the words to express their inner experiences.

At an early age, children often express emotions through actions, not language. A simple but powerful way to help is by inviting your child to make a face or act out how they're feeling. Once they do, you can offer words to match the expression: "That looks like frustration" or "Are you feeling sad right now?" Over time, they begin to connect internal emotions with the vocabulary needed to express them.

This skill is often overlooked because we tend to focus on the behavior, like the tantrum or the tears, rather than the unmet need underneath. Many emotional outbursts come from a lack of communication, not misbehavior. When children can't express what they're feeling, they often act out instead. That's where we come in ~ not to correct but to guide.

If your child struggles to verbalize how they feel, you can introduce alternative forms of communication. Use smiley and frowny face charts, emotion cards, or ask them to point to a picture that represents how they feel. Talk about your own feelings so your child can see them: "I'm feeling a little tired right now," or "You seem upset ~ can you show me how you feel?"

By consistently helping your child identify and name their emotions, you create a more understanding, less reactive environment. You also give them the tools to manage emotions in healthier, more constructive ways ~ now and throughout life.

Here's a categorized list of feelings you can use to begin this practice with your child:

BASIC: Happy, Sad, Angry Scared
LIGHT: Pleasant, Excited, Loved, Proud, Confident, Calm
HEAVY: Unpleasant, Frustrated, Disappointed, Lonely, Hurt, Blamed, Embarrassed
SCARY: Afraid, Anxious, Stressed, Overwhelmed
SOCIAL: Shy, Leftout, Included, Friendly
PHYSICAL: Tired, Restless, Hungry, Energetic
COMPLEX: Ashamed, Resentful, Grateful, Nervous, Confused, Curious, Respectful, Uncomfortable, Comfortable, Motivated, Content

Activity:

Fun and Creative Ways to Teach Emotions

Helping our children learn to recognize and express their emotions doesn't have to feel like a lesson ~ it can be a joyful, playful experience. Here are several hands-on activities you can try at home to make emotional learning fun and interactive:

1. Identify Feelings Jar: Take a glass or plastic jar and fill it with small slips of paper, each labeled with a different emotion. Take turns drawing a feeling from the jar. Once a feeling is chosen, encourage your child to either express that emotion through a facial expression or body movement, or share a time when they felt that way. You can model this by going first to help them feel comfortable.

2. Feelings Tree: Draw or print a tree outline, and cut out leaves using colored paper. On one side of each leaf, write the name of an emotion. On the other side, add a visual cue ~ an emoji face, a picture from a magazine, or a hand-drawn expression. This activity is especially helpful for children who can't yet read or spell. When your child is feeling something but doesn't want to talk, they can simply place the corresponding leaf on the tree. This lets you know how they're feeling without pressure, and you can gently check in by saying, "I see you're feeling ___ I'm here when you are ready to talk."

3. Candy Hearts Game: Fill a jar with candy hearts or any small treats that have short phrases or emotions written on them. Take turns pulling one out. Before anyone gets to eat the candy, they must express the emotion or phrase aloud and talk about a moment they felt that way. It adds a sweet reward to a meaningful conversation.

4. Jelly Bean Emotions: Assign an emotion to each jelly bean color (e.g., red = angry, yellow = happy, green = calm, blue = sad). Have your child pick a jelly bean and describe a time they felt that emotion. Then, they get to eat it! This colorful activity blends sensory play with emotional awareness in a fun, low-pressure way.

5. Feelings Chart with Faces: Create a simple feelings chart using printed smiley, neutral, and frowny faces. Post it in a visible spot, like the fridge or their bedroom wall. When your child struggles to express how they feel, encourage them to point to a face on the chart. Over time, this visual support can help them build the language skills and confidence to verbalize their emotions.

These small, everyday activities can go a long way in helping your child build emotional intelligence. They don't just make learning about feelings easier ~ they make it memorable and meaningful, too.

LET YOUR CHILD GROW

Letting our children discover who they truly are and giving them the space to grow into their unique selves, is one of the greatest gifts we can offer. When we try to control them or mold them into who we think they should be, we limit their potential. We shrink their world instead of expanding it. This kind of control may come from love, but it can end up keeping them small, uncertain, and disconnected from their true identity.

Think of your child like a seed. If you plant it without water, sun, space, or nourishment, it will wither. With patient and consistent care, it grows into something vibrant and life-giving. A healthy plant adds beauty to the world and contributes to the life cycle. Just like when we nurture our children in ways that honor their individuality, we help them bloom into who they are meant to be. In doing so, they bring their own special "oxygen" into the world, offering something only they can give.

When we burden our children with the weight of our expectations or force them to conform to societal norms that don't fit, we rob them of the chance to discover their own purpose. This can leave them feeling lost, unseen, and unsure of their worth. Rather than pushing them to become who we imagine they should be, let's choose to walk beside them as they discover who they already are. Our role is not to steer them into our vision, but to love and support them as they find their own. When we do this, we give them the freedom to flourish ~ to shine in ways that not only fulfill them but also light up the world around them.

Food for Thought

Loving our child means embracing them exactly as they are ~ not as a reflection of our hopes or fears, but as their own person. Sometimes, the need to shape who they become comes from our own unhealed places ~ the dreams we didn't live, or the love we had to earn. When we notice this, we can let go of old patterns and give our children the freedom to grow into themselves.

Ask yourself: Am I nurturing who my child truly is ~ or who I once needed to be?

Let them... Be.

Let them find themselves ~ For they will find glee.

Explore ~ For they will find more.

Let them create with their own eyes ~ For they will take you by surprise.

Let your child walk beyond the veil of conformity.

Let them uncover the brilliance that lies beneath the surface of structure and routine.

Trust their journey. Let them be.

GIVE YOUR CHILD THE TOOLS THEY NEED TO THRIVE IN LIFE

Helping our children thrive starts long before they can speak or read. It begins with how we show up for them ~ noticing their feelings, responding with care, and creating a space where they feel safe being exactly who they are.

The most important tools for life aren't things we can hand to them. They are the everyday habits, ways of thinking, and ways of being that help our children feel capable, confident, and connected.

We can support them in learning:

- **Understanding Their Feelings:** Every feeling matters. Helping our children put words to what they feel and showing them it's okay to express emotions teaches them to handle life instead of fearing it.
- **Knowing Their Worth:** Children need to feel they are enough ~ not for what they do, but for who they are. Celebrating their uniqueness helps them grow into themselves.
- **Setting Boundaries and Respecting Others:** Learning to say "no," speak up, and honor others builds confidence and self-respect.
- **Communicating and Connecting:** Taking the time to listen and respond with empathy shows them that their voice matters.
- **Trusting Themselves and Problem-Solving:** Letting them make choices and gently guiding them through mistakes helps them believe, "I can figure this out."
- **Exploring and Staying Curious:** Encouraging questions, trying new things, and learning from experience helps children see the world as something to discover, not fear.
- **Showing Kindness and Compassion:** When we practice empathy and kindness ~ to themselves, others, and even challenges ~ they learn how to relate and care.
- **Finding Calm and Perspective:** Helping them pause, notice the world, and reflect quietly teaches grounding, balance, and gratitude.
- **Asking for Help When Needed:** Letting them know it's okay to seek support builds strength, not dependence.

When we guide our children in these ways from the very beginning, we help them grow into adults where they feel safe, confident, connected, and brave enough to be themselves.

Activities:

Simple Ways to Give Your Child Emotional Tools

Here are a few easy and meaningful ways to help your child explore their feelings, build confidence, and express themselves:

1. Emotion Jars

Create a set of jars with small objects ~ like colored beads, buttons, or stones ~ where each color represents a feeling (for example, red for anger, blue for sadness, yellow for happiness). Throughout the day, ask your child to drop an object in the jar that matches how they're feeling.

This isn't about getting it "right" ~ it's about noticing and naming feelings. Emotion jars can be a calming tool, a conversation starter, or a gentle way to check in on their day. You can even do it together, showing that it's normal to notice and share your emotions.

2. Celebration Wall

Set up a Celebration Wall at home to highlight acts of courage, kindness, or trying something new. Let your child add notes, drawings, stickers, or symbols whenever they do something that makes them proud ~ like helping a friend, asking a question, or speaking up.

Seeing these moments displayed reinforces their strengths and individuality. Over time, the wall becomes a living reminder that bravery and growth come in many forms, and that every effort matters.

3. Mindfulness Moments

Spend a few quiet minutes each day practicing simple breathing exercises or sharing one thing you're grateful for. These little pauses help children notice their inner world, manage stress, and return to calm when emotions feel big. Doing this together models self-awareness and teaches that taking a moment is always okay.

4. Creative Outlets

Encourage self-expression through art, music, storytelling, or journaling. Drawing, singing, writing, or acting out feelings gives children a safe way to explore and communicate what's happening inside them, even when words feel hard. You can join in too ~ sharing your own creations shows that feelings are meant to be expressed, not hidden.

Reflective Questions

- When my child expresses a strong emotion, how do I respond? Do I listen fully, or do I try to fix it?
- Which of these activities could we do together today to notice, celebrate, or express feelings?
- Are there ways I'm unintentionally comparing or judging my child instead of celebrating who they are?
- How can I practice noticing and naming my own feelings alongside them, showing that it's safe to share and explore emotions at any age?

BUILDING CONFIDENCE THROUGH INSPIRATIONAL TEACHING

Inspirational Learning

When it comes to meaningful learning, our children thrive in spaces where they feel safe to make mistakes and try again; without fear of criticism. Encouragement builds the foundation for growth. When a child feels supported instead of judged, they stay curious, motivated, and open to learning.

One of the most powerful ways to nurture this growth is through what I call the *Connect~Guide~Celebrate* approach: begin with a kind, validating comment, offer gentle guidance, and close with encouragement that reminds them of their effort and progress.

Imagine your child is learning to tie their shoes. You might say, "You're doing a great job ~ learning this takes practice, and I love how you're sticking with it." Then, as you guide them, you could add, "I noticed the loops got a little loose. Try pulling them a bit tighter this time, and see what happens." Finally, you might end with, "You're getting the hang of it. Good job. You're doing amazing."

Moments like these remind children that effort matters as much as the outcome. They learn that mistakes are simply part of the process; not something to be ashamed of. When correction is wrapped in warmth, children feel safe to keep trying.

Make space for learning to feel inspiring, filled with curiosity, wonder, and connection. Ask questions like, "What do you think makes that work?" or "Why do you think that happened?" Let them explore, imagine, and discover answers alongside you.

Be specific when giving directions so they can learn to follow steps with confidence. For example, instead of saying, "Go get the glue," you could say, "The glue is on the middle shelf in the kitchen cabinet; the one with the blue cap." Clear guidance helps avoid frustration and builds real-world problem-solving skills.

If they struggle or can't find something, return to connection first. Connect, guide, and celebrate. Each moment becomes a chance to show patience, understanding, and support.

Let's make learning a shared adventure. It's not about teaching perfection ~ it's about sparking curiosity, joy, and confidence.

Activity:

Shared Learning Experiment

Try learning something new *together*. Bake a new recipe, build a small project, or explore a simple science experiment. Let the process lead the way. Talk about what worked, what didn't, and what you both discovered. End with reflection on what you enjoyed or found surprising.

When learning becomes a shared journey, children see that it's okay not to know everything. What matters most is the willingness to try, learn, and grow side by side.

How I Bring This to Life at Home

I include my children in everyday tasks ~ whether I'm changing the furnace filter or checking the oil in the car. I invite them to watch, never forcing or rushing them. When they're ready, I let them try. I guide with patience, correct gently when needed, and always end with encouragement.

These moments aren't just chores ~ they're confidence builders. I explain why each step matters, ask questions that spark curiosity, and celebrate what they notice or learn. Sometimes frustration shows up, for them or for me. When it does, I pause, take a breath, and remember what it felt like to learn as a child. I remind myself that each child moves at their own pace, and that patience, empathy, and clear guidance create trust.

Of course, I haven't always been perfect ~ there have been times I've lost my patience, my child got upset, and we had to talk about it. She once told me, "I don't learn that way," and I learned from that too. We are all learning together. There will be moments when you, too, feel frustrated or overreact ~ so give yourself grace, apologize to your child, and move forward.

When we approach both our own mistakes and our children's with understanding, we set the stage for a learning environment rooted in trust and curiosity.

By keeping this perspective, we build a space where mistakes are expected, curiosity is welcomed, and learning feels shared rather than pressured. Our children grow best when they feel safe to explore, when we honor their pace, and when love and learning walk hand in hand.

ENCOURAGEMENT

Encouraging our children to be creative, to explore, and to embrace independence is essential for their well-being and for their journey toward discovering who they truly are. Creativity gives them room to express themselves freely and to trust their own ideas. Exploration opens their minds to new experiences and perspectives. Independence builds courage, self-trust, and the confidence to make choices and learn from them.

Together, these three elements ~ creativity, exploration, and independence ~ shape a child's sense of identity and purpose. These qualities become the inner framework that help them grow into who they already are on the inside.

Encouragement is not about pushing or expecting perfection. It grows through presence, patience, and the quiet confidence that trying, stumbling, and rising again are all welcome and safe.

Parents often imagine a path for their children long before they know what they enjoy. Many little moments can surprise us as children discover joy in places we never expected. A child who walks past a soccer field without interest might come alive the moment they pick up a paintbrush or discover music. Their excitement becomes a clue ~ an invitation to lean in with curiosity and ask, "What is it about this that lights you up?" Following their spark opens space for discovery and self-expression that no plan could predict.

Children do not always know what they like or dislike right away. Discovering this takes time, freedom, and space to experiment. Moments of trying something new are not about meeting expectations. These moments help them learn who they are, what feels right, and what makes them feel alive. Encouragement grows whenever we honor their instincts and follow their natural interests rather than guiding them toward a path we imagined for them.

Emotional encouragement matters just as much. Every time you let your child try without pressure, every time you celebrate effort over outcome, and every time you give them room to make their own choices, you are teaching them that their voice matters. Their ideas matter. Their feelings matter. These messages strengthen confidence, resilience, and self-trust ~ the foundation for discovering who they are and who they can become.

Activities:

Encouragement grows when children feel trusted, capable, and supported. These activities give them small, meaningful moments to practice bravery, creativity, and self-belief. Each one strengthens independence while reminding them that their ideas, choices, and efforts matter.

1. The Courage & Curiosity Jar

This activity strengthens bravery, creativity, self-trust, and the willingness to explore new experiences.

What You'll Need:

- One jar or container
- Small slips of paper
- A pen or marker

How to Do It

1. Label the container **Courage & Curiosity**.
2. Write simple challenges on the slips of paper.
3. Fold each slip and place it inside the jar.
4. Invite your child to choose one challenge daily or weekly.
5. Encourage effort, presence, and intention during each challenge.
6. Celebrate the courage it takes to try something new.

Challenge Ideas

- Try something new today
- Learn one new fact
- Create a silly song, dance, or drawing
- Lead the way on a walk
- Taste a new food
- Ask a question you have never asked
- Help with a grown-up task

A clear message grows in their heart:
"You are brave. You can try. I believe in you."

2. The Creativity Corner

This activity gives your child a safe, open-ended space to explore imagination, express feelings, and discover their ideas independently.

What You'll Need:

- A small section of a room
- A basket or shelf for supplies
- Materials such as:
    - paper, crayons, markers, pencils
    - building blocks or loose parts
    - nature items like leaves, rocks, or flowers
    - musical instruments
    - costume pieces or fabrics
    - puzzles or open-ended toys

How to Create It

1. Choose a small area in your home for the creativity space.
2. Place the materials where your child can reach them independently.
3. Offer one guiding message: **There is no wrong way to create here.**
4. Step back and let your child decide what to use and how to use it.
5. Allow them to choose whether to share their creation or keep it private.
6. Praise curiosity, expression, and effort instead of outcome.

A powerful message grows with every choice they make:
"Your ideas matter. Your imagination matters. You matter."
Encouragement grows in the quiet, everyday moments when we choose to believe in our children's potential and support who they are becoming. Creativity, exploration, and independence flourish when children feel safe to try, free to imagine, and valued for their unique

ideas. Every small invitation ~ to experiment, to choose, to discover ~ strengthens their sense of self and gives them room to grow with confidence.

These simple activities offer gentle ways to nurture that growth. Each moment of curiosity, courage, or creativity becomes a seed planted in their hearts. Over time, those seeds grow into trust, resilience, and a deeper understanding of themselves. Encouragement is not a single act; it is a way of showing up, day by day, with openness and belief. When children feel this kind of support, they carry it with them into every corner of their lives, knowing they are capable, worthy, and free to become who they truly are.

QUALITY TIME

Spending quality time with our children holds more value than any gift, vacation, or flashy experience. While those things can bring temporary joy, it's the day-to-day presence, conversations, and moments of connection that shape a child's emotional world. Children flourish when they feel seen, heard, and truly understood. That sense of security and belonging isn't built through occasional grand gestures ~ it's built through consistent, meaningful time together.

When we prioritize time with our children, we send a clear message:

You matter. Not because of what you do or what you achieve, but simply because of who you are.

These shared moments play a powerful role in developing your child's communication skills, self-esteem, empathy, respect, and trust. When you give your full attention ~ without phones, distractions, or multitasking ~ it creates space for honest conversations. Your child feels safe to open up, to ask questions, to be themselves. This builds confidence and deepens your connection. Through these interactions, your child also learns empathy by watching how you listen, how you respond, and how you honor their feelings.

Spending time together regularly teaches mutual respect. When your child sees that their thoughts, ideas, and interests matter to you, they begin to value themselves more. Over time, these moments create an unshakable sense of trust; trust that you are their safe place, no matter what.

Communicating effectively with our children takes effort, patience, and presence. It starts with knowing them ~ not just as your child, but as a unique individual. Some children are talkative and expressive. Others are more quiet and reflective. Time spent together helps you learn their language ~ what comforts them, what triggers them, what excites them.

Involve your child in your daily life. Let them help with cooking, fixing things, or running errands. These small, shared tasks create a natural space for connection without pressure. Open up during these moments; share your thoughts, explain how something works, and tell a story. These small exchanges build comfort and familiarity.

Showing up matters, too. Attend their performances, games, and milestones. Cheer for their wins. Be there during their losses. These moments, big and small, communicate one simple truth: *You are a priority in my life.*

Activity:

Here are some meaningful ways to spend quality time with your child that strengthen connection, communication, and trust:

1. One-on-One Time: Set aside time just for the two of you ~ no phones, no siblings, no distractions. Let your child decide what to do: a walk, a meal, a game, or a craft. Follow their lead. By letting them choose, you show them that their interests' matter. This time doesn't have to be elaborate. What matters most is that it's consistent and uninterrupted.

2. Build Meaningful Routines: Create small traditions ~ Saturday morning pancakes, Sunday evening walks, or a weekly movie night. These routines provide stability, and over time, they become safe spaces for open conversations. Shared rituals offer comfort and build long-term connections.

3. Encourage Creative Expression: Do something creative together ~ draw, write stories, paint, or journal side by side. These activities help children express emotions that may be hard to verbalize. If your child draws something or writes a story, ask about it. Their creations often hold hidden feelings or thoughts they're not yet ready to say out loud.

4. Bedtime Chats: At the end of the day, when everything quiets down, children often feel more open. Use this time to talk gently about their day. Ask open-ended questions like, "What was the best part of your day?" or "Is there anything on your mind before bed?" These moments build trust and emotional intimacy.

5. Practice Active Listening: When your child talks, stop what you're doing. Make eye contact. Don't interrupt. Just listen. When they finish, acknowledge their emotions; even if you don't agree. "That sounds frustrating," or "I hear you; it makes sense why you'd feel that way." Validation builds trust and encourages them to keep opening up.

6. Stay Curious: Ask thoughtful questions that invite more than yes-or-no answers. Instead of "Did you have a good day?" "What made you smile today?" or "What challenged you today?" Your curiosity shows your child they are worth knowing ~ every part of them.

By consistently investing time in these ways, you do more than create good memories ~ you build a solid emotional foundation that will carry your child through every stage of life. You teach them what a real connection looks like. You show them that love is *presence* and that presence is what they'll remember most.

FREEDOM OF EXPRESSION

Granting our children the freedom to express themselves is one of the most powerful ways we can nurture their self-confidence, self-love, and self-esteem. When children feel safe to share their thoughts, emotions, and creativity ~ without fear of criticism or punishment ~ they begin to trust their inner voice. They learn that their feelings are valid, that their opinions matter, and that they have something valuable to contribute. This sense of safety builds emotional strength and teaches them to stand confidently in who they are.

Encouraging expression not only reinforces a child's sense of worth, but it also allows them to fully embrace their individuality. When children are free to explore and communicate their inner world, they begin to uncover what brings them joy, what stirs their imagination, and what lights up their spirit. These moments of discovery often lead them to their passions and strengths, which, in turn, foster a deep sense of purpose.

When we honor our children's need to express themselves, we're not just allowing them to be creative, we're giving them permission to be *real*. We're creating the foundation for authenticity, courage, and lasting happiness. Children who feel free to be themselves are more adaptable, more confident, and better equipped to chase their dreams and navigate life's challenges.

Activity:

Here are some engaging ways to support self-expression in your child ~ each one designed to build confidence, creativity, and emotional awareness:

1. Creative Arts: Give your child access to a variety of materials ~ paper, paints, clay, markers, recyclables ~ and simply let them create. Don't guide or correct them. Don't tell them what to make. Just observe and celebrate what emerges. Whether it's a messy painting or an abstract sculpture, this freedom to explore without rules builds trust in one's own instincts and abilities.

2. Role-Playing and Storytelling: Set up pretend scenarios ~ playing school, running a restaurant, going on a treasure hunt ~ or invent characters together and build stories around them. These playful activities encourage emotional exploration, empathy, and imagination. They also allow children to express complex thoughts in ways that feel fun and safe.

3. Music and Dance: Encourage your child to sing loudly, drum on pots and pans, choreograph silly dances, or simply move their body to music. Music is a universal outlet for emotion, and dancing freely allows children to release energy, process feelings, and connect with their bodies in a joyful way. Try creating a family dance night where everyone joins in without judgment.

4. Choice-Based Exploration: Let your child decide what activities they want to try ~ whether it's soccer, painting, robotics, or gardening. Give them space to start something new and the freedom to change their mind. This freedom helps them discover their interests and build self-awareness without being boxed into anyone else's expectations.

5. Free Play: Sometimes, the best thing you can do is *nothing*. Give your child time and space to play however they want; without an agenda, without screens, and without adult direction. Free play allows creativity, problem-solving, independence, and joy. It's where self-expression comes to life in its purest form.

By consistently offering these kinds of open, judgment-free opportunities for self-expression, you send your child a powerful message: *You are free to be you. Your ideas matter. Your creativity is valuable. Your voice deserves to be heard.*

This freedom helps them not only discover who they are, but also love who they are becoming.

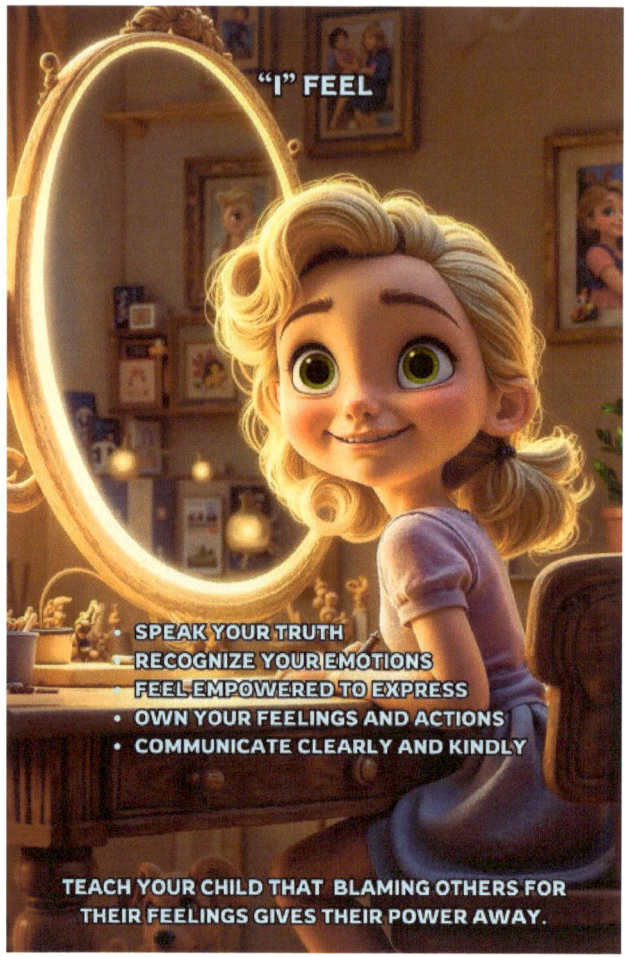

"I" FEEL

Teaching our children to say "I feel" instead of "You make me feel" is a powerful step toward building empowerment, emotional intelligence, self-awareness, and accountability. When children say, "You make me feel," they unintentionally hand over their emotional power. They place the responsibility for how they feel into someone else's hands, which not only creates blame but also disempowers them from understanding or managing their emotions.

By shifting the language to **"I feel,"** we help our children notice and name their emotions. This simple habit shows them that feelings come from inside, often shaped by their own thoughts, beliefs, or past experiences. When they pay attention to how something affects them, they can start to explore why. Sometimes, what they're feeling isn't really about what's happening right now ~ it might come from an old hurt, an expectation they have, or a belief they didn't even realize they were carrying.

Helping children connect with their emotions and understand where they come from teaches them to pause before reacting. They can start asking, *"Is this feeling about what's happening now, or is it coming from something deeper?"* This gives them the chance to respond in new ways: pause and breathe, name the feeling, notice the cause, express it safely, ask for support, or choose a response that fits the moment. Over time, they learn that their emotions aren't something to fear or push away, but something to notice, understand, and grow from.

As children learn to express themselves with "I feel" statements, they naturally build more respectful and effective communication skills. Instead of blaming or pointing the finger at others, they begin to voice their emotions with clarity and empathy ~ skills that will support them not just in childhood but throughout life.

Encouraging emotional honesty helps our children develop a strong sense of self ~ one that isn't defined by the expectations or projections of others. As they learn to trust their own voice and understand their emotions, they begin to make choices that reflect who they truly are. Over time, they come to see that their emotions are not something to fear or suppress, but to listen to, understand, and grow from.

Activities:

Helping Children Notice and Share Their Feelings

1. Journaling or Writing: Give your child a journal or notebook as their own space to write freely ~ stories, poems, or thoughts about their day. Encourage them to start some entries with "I feel..." and explore what's happening inside. This simple habit helps them pause, reflect, and put feelings into words.

You might suggest prompts like:

- "Today, I felt ___ because..."
  - "When ___ happened, I noticed I felt..."
  - "Is this feeling really mine, or is it something I've been told I should feel?"

2. Creative Expression: Older children or teens can try expressing emotions through art, music, or writing ~ short stories, plays, or even a blog. It gives them a safe, creative way to explore what they're feeling and find the words to share it.

3. Open Conversations: Make space for gentle, judgment-free talks. You can start by sharing your own feelings, for example, "I feel frustrated when..." or "I feel proud because..." This shows that all feelings are okay and that talking about them is normal.

4. Listening and Validation: When your child talks about how they feel, focus on being present rather than fixing things. Acknowledge their experience with phrases like, "It sounds like you felt left out," or "I hear that you were excited, and it didn't go the way you hoped." Feeling understood helps them trust themselves and feel safe opening up.

5. Feelings Tools: Simple tools like an **emotions chart or "I feel..."** **cards** can help children put feelings into words. Use them during calm moments, after disagreements, or at bedtime check-ins. These small aids remind your child that it's okay to notice and share what's going on inside.

"I Feel..." Emotion Cards Activity

What You'll Need

- A marker or pen
- Small index cards or sticky notes
- A small box, basket, or envelope to hold the cards

- Optional: Blank cards for your child to create their own emotions

Setup

1. Choose 8–12 core emotions to start with.
2. Examples: Happy, Sad, Frustrated, Excited, Anxious, Proud, Angry, Disappointed, Calm, Confused, Silly, Nervous.
3. Write one emotion on each card in big, easy-to-read letters.
4. Place all the cards in a small box or basket.
5. Add 3–5 blank cards for your child to create their own words or drawings.

Steps:

1. Introduce the cards during a calm moment.

You might say: "These are our 'I feel...' cards. They help us share how our hearts feel inside."

2. Have your child look through the cards.

Encourage curiosity: "Which feelings do you recognize? Which ones look interesting?"

3. Ask them to choose a card that matches their feeling.

If they're unsure, offer gentle support: "Does your heart feel more calm or more frustrated right now?"

4. If none fit, invite them to make their own.

Let them draw a face or symbol - this helps ownership and expression.

5. Use the card as a conversation opener.

Ask simple, grounded questions:

- "What caused this feeling? What happened?"
- "What does your body feel like when this happens?"
- "What do you need right now?"

6. Repeat this often - during calm moments, after disagreements, or at bedtime.

The more you use the cards, the safer and easier emotional expression becomes.

DOES YOUR CHILD FEEL SAFE? EMOTIONALLY?

Knowing if our children feel emotionally safe starts with quiet observation ~ paying attention to how they act, talk, and respond day to day. Emotional safety isn't always something they can put into words, but it shows in how they relate to you and others.

A child who feels safe will share their thoughts and feelings openly, come to you when they're upset, and express themselves without fear of being shut down. They're often willing to try new things, even if they're unsure, because they trust that mistakes won't change your love or approval. You'll see confidence in their words, actions, and choices.

If a child doesn't feel safe, they might pull away. They may hesitate to speak up, become defensive, or avoid conversations altogether. Some act out with anger or frustration; others shut down and grow quiet or anxious. A child who worries about being judged or misunderstood might avoid eye contact, tell small lies, or constantly seek reassurance. These behaviors aren't about being "difficult" ~ they're signs that your child may need more emotional safety and connection.

Creating Emotional Safety

Creating emotional safety for our children doesn't require perfection. It comes from being present, patient, and showing your child ~ again and again ~ that they are loved, valued, and safe to be themselves, even when their feelings are messy or uncomfortable. It also means being reliable, keeping our word, and showing up when we say we will. Emotional safety grows when we listen without judgment, respect boundaries, stay calm during their struggles, and respond with understanding and care. It's in these everyday moments that children learn they can trust us, be honest, make mistakes, and still feel supported.

Activity:

Emotional Safety Check-In

Ask a question that goes a little deeper than "How was your day?" Some ideas:

- "Is there anything you've been scared to tell me?"
- "Do you ever feel like I don't understand you?"
- "What's something you wish I knew about how you feel?"
- "Do you feel safe talking to me when something's bothering you?"

If they hesitate or avoid answering, don't push. See it as a chance to pause and reflect. It may mean your connection needs a little strengthening ~ and that's okay. Gently reassure them:

"It's okay if it's hard to talk. I'm here, and I want to understand you better. We can grow together."

Emotional safety is built in small, everyday moments through consistency, kindness, and honest connection. Showing up this way lets your child know it's safe to be fully themselves, even when life or feelings get messy.

Food For Thought

This is your opportunity to help your child not just feel loved, but also to learn how to love and accept themselves. Childhood is the most powerful time to lay this foundation, so that when your child steps into adulthood, they carry with them confidence, emotional strength, and a quiet sense of inner peace. Above all, they'll know they are never alone on this journey ~ that someone has seen them, believed in them, and walked beside them every step of the way.

TEACHING VS CRITIQUING

As parents, our role isn't to point out flaws ~ it's to guide, support, and cheer our children on. Approaching parenting like a teacher rather than a critic helps our children grow while building their confidence and sense of self. Celebrating effort, noticing strengths, and seeing challenges as chances to learn matters far more than focusing on mistakes.

Criticism, even when we don't intend it, can leave a mark. Harsh words or repeated judgment can make a child feel unseen, afraid to try, or unsure of themselves. Parenting as a teacher means walking beside our children with patience and care. It means offering guidance without shame and reminding them that mistakes are simply part of lcarning.

I often think of a friend I grew up with whose father didn't guide that way. His approach centered on critique rather than teaching. Nothing ever felt quite good enough, and the focus stayed on what was wrong instead of what was done well.

I don't believe his father meant harm. He simply didn't have the awareness or patience to slow down and notice the good. My friend grew up feeling small and unintelligent, and those feelings followed him into adulthood. He struggled with unworthiness, turned to alcohol, and carried a lifelong sense of never measuring up. He lost touch with who he truly was because he spent so many years trying to fit into a version of himself his father imagined. Even now, healing feels overwhelming for him.

I think of him often as a reminder of how powerful our words and tone can be. A gentler, more teaching-centered approach might have shaped his confidence, identity, and sense of possibility in very different ways.

Creating a safe space for our children allows them to explore, experiment, and take risks without fear. When they feel supported instead of judged, curiosity grows. Confidence builds. Their efforts start to feel meaningful, not just the final result.

When our children share something they've created ~ a drawing, story, project, or idea ~ they're offering a piece of themselves. They're showing trust and believing we'll meet them with care. Even on tired or rushed days, we can pause long enough to see the effort, thought, and courage it took to share. If there's a chance to offer guidance, we can do it gently, planting it as an idea for next time so their excitement stays alive.

These little exchanges become a mirror, not only showing our children how we see them, but showing them how we see ourselves as learners too.

Children learn just as much from how we treat ourselves. Showing patience, kindness, and a willingness to grow teaches them to approach their own mistakes with the same compassion. Parenting as a teacher creates a home where curiosity is welcomed, learning is ongoing, and every child feels capable, seen, and supported.

As we practice this approach, it helps to pause once in a while and check in with ourselves. These moments of reflection keep us grounded in the kind of parent we want to be.

Pause and ask yourself:

- What happens in my child's body language when I respond with warmth rather than correction?

- How do I speak to myself when *I* make a mistake? Would I want my child to use that same tone with themselves?

- Where can I slow down, even briefly, to notice effort instead of rushing to the result?

- What moments this week invited me to guide gently instead of critique quickly?

- How do I want my child to feel when they share something with me? Does my reaction match that intention?

These quiet check-ins help us stay present. They remind us that parenting as a teacher is less about getting everything right and more about showing up with awareness, softness, and a willingness to grow alongside our children. When we carry that mindset into the moments we share with them, it becomes easier to slow down, explore together, and make space for curiosity to lead the way.

Activity:

Explore Together

Set aside special time a few times a month to explore something your child is curious about. Let them pick the topic or skill ~ drawing, building, cooking, a new game ~ and guide gently as they try it on their own. Celebrate their effort, the questions they ask, and the small discoveries they make.

Focus on learning, not the result. Keep it relaxed and fun. Sit side by side, ask curious questions, and notice the little steps our children figure out on their own. Laugh at mistakes, celebrate small wins, and remind ourselves ~ and them ~that it's okay not to get it perfect. At home, it's the journey ~ the trying, exploring, and discovering ~ that matters most. By staying present and encouraging them every step of the way, we show that they are safe, capable, and deeply loved.

HOW DO YOU GET YOUR CHILD TO OPEN UP AND TALK TO YOU?

Building a strong, open relationship with our children starts with creating a home where trust, respect, and understanding guide everyday moments. To help them feel safe sharing what's on their minds, we need to spend real, meaningful time together, speak honestly, and try to see the world through their eyes. When a child opens their heart to us, it's a gift ~ a reminder that our presence matters more than we often realize.

Children need to know they can rely on us. Trust grows slowly, through small, consistent actions: keeping our promises, following through on what we say, and showing that our words carry weight. Calm, respectful communication reinforces that their thoughts and feelings matter. When we respond with patience instead of anger, we send the message that it's safe to express themselves and that they are valued.

At the same time, we want to actively meet our children where they are. That means literally getting down to their level ~ sitting on the floor, kneeling beside them, or crouching at eye level ~ so they feel seen and understood. It means asking about the things that matter to them: their favorite toy or game and why it's special, the friends who are important to them, or what makes them laugh and feel alive. By showing genuine interest and curiosity, we help our children open up in ways that build connection far beyond rules and boundaries.

Exploring their interests alongside them is powerful. Play with them, ask questions about what they enjoy, share in their discoveries, and celebrate the small details they notice. These moments of presence ~ eye-to-eye, heart-to-heart ~ tell them: I see you. I want to understand you. Even when we don't fully get it at first, the effort itself shows that we care deeply and are committed to understanding them.

Part of creating this safe space is letting them see the real us. Sharing our own struggles, mistakes, and growth shows that being human is about learning, evolving, and staying honest with ourselves. My children know the choices I regret, the times I doubted myself, and the ways I'm still learning. By showing our authentic selves, we invite them to do the same ~ to be honest, vulnerable, curious, and fully themselves.

When relationships are built on trust, understanding, and presence, our children learn they can share their world with us. They discover that we will meet them there with love, attention, patience, and genuine interest. In those shared moments ~ laughing, asking, listening, and exploring ~ we create a connection that supports not just their emotional safety, but their sense of wonder, curiosity, and confidence to be exactly who they are.

Activities:

Building Closeness Together

1. Reflection & Connection

Take a quiet moment to think about your own journey. What parts of your past could help your child feel closer to you? Consider sharing:

- A mistake you made and what it taught you
- A time you struggled with self-doubt or fear
- How you've grown or are still learning today

Share your story calmly and honestly, free from shame. Invite your child to ask questions or share their own feelings. Showing them that being human means making mistakes and growing together creates trust and deepens your connection.

2. Active Listening Game

Take turns sharing a short story or moment from your day. After one person shares, the listener repeats back what they heard using phrases like, "So what you're saying is..." or "Let me make sure I got that right..."

This game teaches listening with empathy and shows your child that their voice matters. Practicing it regularly strengthens trust, encourages openness, and helps them feel safe sharing deeper emotions. Over time, it builds confidence and a relationship with us, grounded in understanding and support.

UNDERSTANDING YOUR CHILD'S PERSPECTIVE

Developing an understanding perspective means making a conscious choice to step into another person's world ~ to see situations through their eyes, and to notice their feelings, experiences, and intentions without judgment. It asks us to practice empathy, openness, and truly listening with care. When we approach others this way, we create space for genuine connection, heartfelt communication, and relationships built on trust and respect.

With our children, this way of seeing is especially powerful. It means paying attention to their thoughts, feelings, and reactions ~ even when they are different from our own ~ and responding with patience, kindness, and care. Children often express themselves in ways that feel unfamiliar or confusing, but their experience is always real and important. By stepping into their world, we affirm who they are, honor their individuality, and show them that their voice matters.

Understanding our children doesn't mean we have to agree with everything they think or do. It simply means recognizing their perspective as real and meaningful. That acknowledgment ~ without judgment ~ builds trust, strengthens our bond, and nurtures a sense of security. It teaches our children that they can share their thoughts openly, that their feelings are valued, and that they are supported in exploring life from their own point of view.

When we practice seeing the world through our children's eyes, we help them grow with confidence, curiosity, and a strong sense of self. We show them that they are heard, seen, and loved exactly as they are; a gift that shapes not only their childhood but the adults they will become.

Activity:

Choose a simple object ~ maybe a rock, a toy, or something from around the house. Ask your child to look at it closely and share what they see, how it makes them feel, what they imagine it could be used for, and whether they find it interesting. Then, take a turn sharing your own thoughts about the same object. Notice the differences in your perspectives and celebrate them together.

This isn't just a fun way to start a conversation; it's a chance to encourage curiosity, creativity, and empathy. Most importantly, it shows your child that their way of seeing the world matters, that their ideas and feelings are valued, and that their voice has a place in your shared space.

Food for Thought

Think back to a time you were a child and shared an idea, thought, or perspective that someone ~ maybe even a parent ~ found funny, strange, or outlandish. How did it feel to be laughed at or not fully understood?

Now, imagine your own child seeing the world in their own unique way. Their perspective might seem unusual or surprising to you, but it makes sense to them. What happens if, instead of correcting or dismissing it, we ask them to explain more? How might it feel to simply honor their way of seeing things, even if we don't fully understand it ourselves?

Reflecting on these moments reminds us that the gift of perspective is seeing the world through someone else's eyes ~ and that our child's way of experiencing life is valuable, simply because it is theirs.

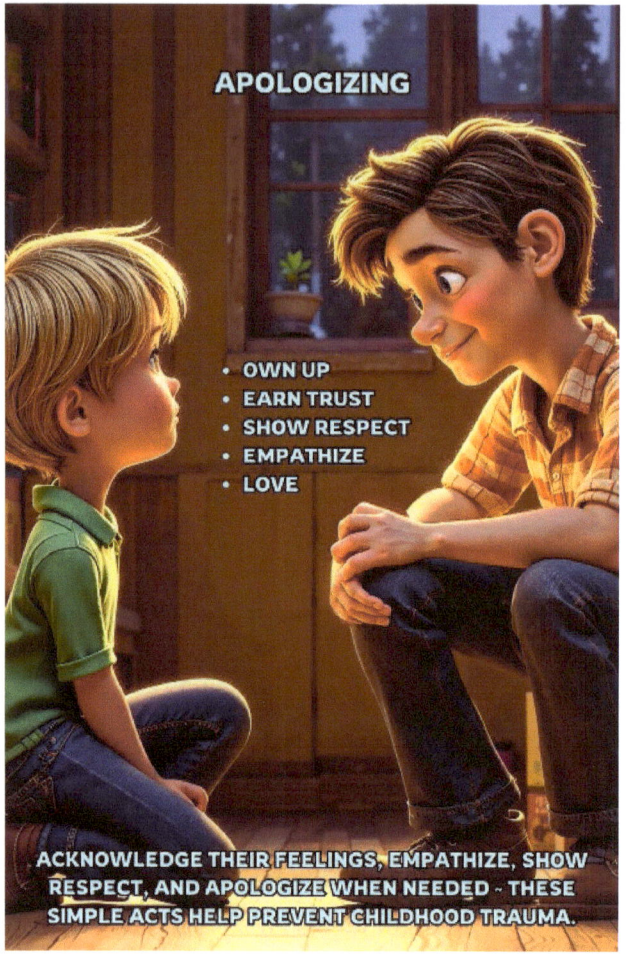

APOLOGIZING

As parents, it's important to take responsibility when we hurt our children ~ through words, actions, or reactions. We're human, and there will be moments when our patience wears thin, we speak carelessly, or we handle a situation poorly. Even a single harsh word can leave a mark, so acknowledging our mistakes becomes an act of love.

Taking the time to apologize and ask for forgiveness sends a powerful message: *your feelings matter, and I see the impact of my actions*. It's important to clarify that what was said in the heat of the moment wasn't true, to explain that our behavior came from our own stress or overwhelm, not from anything they did wrong, and make them aware that it wasn't their fault. This act of humility and accountability teaches our children how to take ownership of their mistakes, seek forgiveness, and mend relationships in healthy ways.

By showing accountability, we teach through example: courage, empathy, and emotional honesty. Our children learn that everyone makes mistakes and that what truly matters is how we respond. They also learn to face their mistakes with kindness and humility, which helps them feel more trusting and connected.

A sincere apology tells our children: *I see you. Your feelings matter. What happened wasn't your fault.* This goes beyond saying "I'm sorry." It's a chance to reflect, reconnect, and show that relationships can be repaired, and love isn't lost when we make mistakes.

A heartfelt apology can include:

- Recognizing what happened and how it affected them: "I can see that what I said hurt you, and I feel awful about that."
- Naming your own emotions without blaming them: "I was feeling overwhelmed, and I reacted in a way that wasn't fair to you."
- Reassuring them of your love: "You are not at fault, and I love you just as you are."

These moments are also opportunities to connect and teach. Listen deeply to their feelings, share your reflections, and discuss ways to handle similar situations in the future. Actions following an apology ~ like hugging, spending time together, or quietly reconnecting ~ can communicate even more than words.

Activity:

Apology and Forgiveness Circle

Find a quiet, cozy spot where you and your child can sit close and feel comfortable. Let them know this is a special time for just the two of you to connect and talk openly.

- **Start by noticing how they're feeling and inviting conversation:**

"I noticed you've seemed upset since [situation], and I want to talk about it."
This shows your child that you see them and that their feelings matter.

- **When it's your turn, offer a genuine apology. Focus on your own actions using "I" statements:**

"I'm sorry for the way I reacted when I said [hurtful words or actions]. I was frustrated, but that doesn't excuse what I did."
Be honest about what you were feeling, and make it clear that your reaction wasn't about them and wasn't their fault. Remind them they are loved and valued no matter what.

- **Then, gently ask for forgiveness:**

"I'm really sorry for hurting you. Will you forgive me?"
Give them time to respond. Listen carefully to how they felt without interrupting or defending yourself.

- **You can reflect back what you hear:**

"It sounds like that really hurt your feelings, and I understand why you felt that way."

- **Finish with something comforting ~ a hug, reading a favorite story, or sitting quietly together. Let the moment end with warmth and connection.**

Food For Thought

Think back to your own childhood. Was there a time a parent or caregiver hurt or let you down and didn't apologize? How did that feel? Do you still feel any of it now ~ anger, sadness, or maybe confusion?

Notice how that experience may have shaped the way you trust others, speak up, or feel about yourself.

Now, imagine offering your child what you may have needed in that moment: a genuine apology, understanding, and the reassurance that mistakes don't mean love is lost. Thinking about this can help you approach your own apologies with heart, presence, and the intention to repair and grow your connection.

LOVE

Love isn't something we can wrap up in a bow or slip into a gift bag. It's something we give through our time, our attention, and our presence. Our children don't measure love in things ~ they feel it in the quiet moments when we stop, listen, and truly see them.

It's easy to believe that new toys, special outings, or surprises show our love ~ and for a moment, they do bring happiness. What a child remembers most, though, isn't the gift itself; it's the person who was there sharing it. The one who gave the hug and said, *"I love you."* Love grows through connection, not entertainment.

Our children learn what love feels like through us. They need to hear it, see it, and experience it in the way we show up day after day. When we sit beside them, listen to their stories, and say, *"I see you. I hear you. I feel you. I love you just as you are,"* something inside them settles. They learn they matter.

Being present doesn't mean filling every moment with activity. It means stepping into their world with curiosity. Sitting next to them while they draw, watching them create, or asking, "How did that make you feel?" These small gestures teach them that who they are is enough.

Love shows itself through empathy. It is the gentle act of acknowledging their feelings without judgment, even when those feelings seem confusing or loud. When we respond with calm understanding, we show that emotions are safe to feel and safe to share.

When love is missing, a child may grow up unsure of what it truly feels like. They might confuse attention with gifts or believe love must be earned. Love is not a transaction. It is the steady willingness to notice, to stay, to care. It is felt in our tone, our patience, our eyes meeting theirs.

Children perceive love through what we do, not only what we say. If we are not there when they need support, if we turn away when they're crying, or if we're often too distracted to notice their needs, they may quietly begin to wonder if they are worthy of love ~ even when our hearts mean something very different. Sometimes even a harsh glance or a rushed response can leave a deeper mark than we realize.

Words like *"I love you"* matter deeply, yet they must be backed by actions that show consistency, care, and safety. Children are remarkably perceptive ~ they feel everything. When they see love lived out through patience, kindness, and respect, they begin to understand what love truly means.

The way we treat others teaches them what love looks like. Every interaction ~ how we speak to our partner, how we respond to a mistake, how we handle frustration ~ becomes part of their education in love. When they see gentleness, empathy, and understanding at home, they grow up knowing that love is steady, safe, and real.

Over time, these small, loving actions build a foundation of security and self-worth. A child who feels consistently loved carries that certainty within them. They no longer have to question their value or chase love elsewhere, because they know, deep down, they already have it.

The most meaningful gift we can ever give isn't something we buy or plan; it's ourselves. Our real, listening, feeling, present selves. When we offer that kind of love, it becomes the language they understand best.

Love is felt. It's remembered. It's what teaches a child to believe, quietly and completely: I am safe. I am seen. I am loved.

Reflection

- When did I last truly listen without distraction?
- How often do I notice my child's unspoken feelings?
- What small moments today could I turn into a memory of connection?
- How can I show love in a way that my child actually feels it?

These questions aren't meant to make you feel bad or point fingers. They're simply a gentle check-in ~ a reminder to pause in the middle of the noise. Life moves fast, and it's easy to get swept up in the long list of things that need to be done. Sometimes we forget how powerful even one quiet moment of connection can be ~ a quick hug before rushing out the door, a few seconds of eye contact that say, *"I'm here with you."* Those small moments hold more meaning than we often realize. Love doesn't require perfection; it just asks that we keep returning to presence, again and again.

Love lives in the moments we choose to slow down, notice, and simply be there.

ACTIVE LISTENING

Active listening is one of the most powerful ways we can support our children's growth and strengthen our connection with them. When we listen with full attention ~ without interrupting, judging, or rushing to respond ~ we send a clear message: *your voice matters*. This kind of listening validates their feelings, honors their experiences, and helps them feel seen and understood.

Accepting our child's perspective, even when it differs from our own, creates a sense of safety. It tells them they are allowed to see the world through their own eyes. Love grows in that space of acceptance. Children don't always need us to agree; they need to know we are willing to hear them. When they sense that their thoughts are welcomed rather than dismissed, their hearts open. They begin to share more honestly, because they trust they won't be shut down or corrected.

Connection deepens in those quiet moments when listening replaces judgment and curiosity takes the place of control. No parent gets it right all the time. We misunderstand, rush, or react. What matters most is returning, again and again, with an open heart and the desire to understand. Every time we try to see through their eyes, we tell our children something they'll never forget: *you are worth understanding.*

As parents, it's natural to want to protect our children or step in to solve their problems. Yet often, the greatest support we can offer is simply to listen. We don't have to fix every hurt or provide every answer. Sometimes our calm presence and willingness to hold space are exactly what they need to find their own clarity. When we listen with patience and guide gently rather than directing, we teach them to trust their own voice.

This kind of listening nurtures confidence, problem-solving, and self-trust. It shows them they are capable and reminds them that their feelings and ideas have value. Over time, this becomes the foundation of independence ~ an inner voice that says, *I can handle this.*

Active listening doesn't just help our children grow; it helps us grow, too. It invites us to slow down, to practice empathy, and to love with deeper understanding. When we approach our children with openness and a willingness to learn alongside them, something shifts. The relationship becomes a partnership built on mutual respect, where both hearts feel heard.

That kind of connection becomes an emotional anchor ~ a safe, steady place our children will carry with them for the rest of their lives.

Activity:

Words That Hold Us

Children need to *hear* this message ~ and *feel* it. Read it aloud to them, especially after a misunderstanding or emotional moment. Let your voice carry calm, warmth, and understanding. These words can become an anchor ~ something they know in their heart even before they fully understand every word.

As your child grows, they can return to these words on their own. They can read them whenever they need comfort, reassurance, or a reminder that they are safe and loved.

If your child can't read yet, they can still learn the meaning through your actions, tone, and presence. You might draw pictures together to represent the words; a heart for love, an ear for listening, open hands for acceptance. If they're learning to read, point to the words as you say them, helping them connect language with emotion.

You can even hang these words somewhere special ~ framed, written on colorful paper, or surrounded by their artwork. Let it become a visible reminder that they are safe, seen, and loved for exactly who they are.

"I hear you. I see you. I'm listening. Your perspective matters, even if I don't fully understand it. This is your experience, your reality, and how you see things is valid. Your feelings are real and important ~ even if I can't relate to them in the same way. I honor that. I won't dismiss or simplify your emotions. I recognize how deeply you feel, and I accept every-thing you're expressing ~ your perspective, your voice, and who you are. I'm here to support you, to love you, and to walk beside you through whatever you're facing. As we go through this together, I'll share what I've learned from my own life, not to tell you what to do but to guide you with love. My goal is for you to feel seen, understood, and empowered ~ knowing that you are never alone."

Read this as often as they need. Read aloud together if they can read. These words build trust, heal misunderstandings, and remind your child that they are never alone.

OPEN DOOR

It can feel scary for a child to worry about disappointing us. That worry can weigh heavily, even when they've done nothing wrong. One of the most important gifts we can offer is the assurance that, no matter what happens, they are always welcome in our hearts. Our arms are open, our attention is ready, and together we will figure things out. Mistakes may have consequences, but those consequences are part of learning and growing ~ never a measure of their worth. This foundation of love creates the safety children need to be open and truthful, even when mistakes happen.

Building on that sense of safety, we can help our children understand that honesty will always be met with care, understanding, and gentle guidance. Talking with them ahead of time, we can make it clear that when mistakes or consequences occur, they will never face them alone. We will be there to support them, help them learn, and walk through each step together. Parenting isn't about perfection; it's about being present, showing up with love, and learning alongside our children as they grow.

Even with the best intentions, we don't always get it right. Sometimes we may react more strongly than we intended, and our children may see that. When it happens, there's an opportunity to take responsibility and make things right. We can acknowledge it, apologize, and explain what we wish we had done differently. For example:

"I know I got upset just now. I wish I had handled it with more calm and understanding. I'm sorry for my reaction, and next time I'll try to step back before responding."

When we make mistakes and take responsibility, we show that everyone is learning, love doesn't go away, and we can always repair what's been broken. How we handle these moments ~ with honesty, reflection, and care ~ matters far more than getting everything perfect.

By handling our own missteps with care, we reinforce the safety for children to share openly, knowing they will be met with understanding rather than judgment. Our children do not need us to agree with everything they share; they just need to feel safe telling the truth. Their willingness to be honest is a sign of trust, and those moments become opportunities to teach, guide, and show what love looks like when it listens and holds space.

Once they feel safe to speak honestly, gentle questions can guide reflection and growth. Asking things like, *"Do you think there was another way to handle that?"* or *"How do you feel about what happened?"* invites reflection without shame. Mistakes become moments of learning, moments of connection. Most importantly, our children need to hear that they are loved ~ always ~ and that their honesty matters far more than getting everything perfect.

An open-door relationship builds trust, emotional safety, and lasting communication. When children know they can speak freely, without fear of anger or judgment, honesty feels safe instead of risky. Connection replaces fear, and understanding replaces control. Learning happens naturally through conversations, shared moments, and gentle guidance.

When mistakes happen, love stays. Guidance replaces anger, reassurance replaces fear, giving children courage to face challenges and confidence to trust themselves. Trust forms the foundation of every strong relationship. Feeling safe to be honest encourages children to share everything: friendships, school pressures, confusing emotions, even serious concerns like bullying or anxiety. They learn that their voice matters and that telling the truth will not cost them love or belonging.

Open, accepting homes shape patterns that last a lifetime. Children raised this way grow into adults who are honest, emotionally aware, and compassionate. This safe foundation also protects them from hiding fears or struggles. Whether facing peer pressure, online challenges, or deeper worries, children can trust that love is steady, hearts are open, and guidance is gentle.

Remind them again and again: no matter what happens, they can always come to us. That reassurance becomes an anchor ~ a safe, steady place to return to, a quiet strength that gives courage to face the world, knowing they never have to walk through it alone.

Activity:

Open Door Moment

Choose a quiet time ~ perhaps during an evening walk, before bed, or while sitting together after dinner ~ when life feels slower and your children are most open to conversation. Begin by reminding them that there is always space in your heart and home for honesty. You might say:

"You can always tell me anything. Even if you think I won't like it, I'll always listen and love you the same."

Invite them to share something small ~ perhaps a worry, a mistake, or something they were afraid to tell you. Listen without interrupting.

Let them feel, through your eyes, tone, and presence, that you are fully there and safe.

If they open up, thank them for trusting you:

"That took a lot of courage to tell me. You were honest, and I hope you can feel proud of yourself for that."

(Note: "I don't say 'I'm proud of you for being honest,' because that can feel like my pride is conditional. Honesty is a learning process, and I want it to feel natural rather than earned, so I focus on helping them feel proud of themselves instead.")

If they aren't ready to talk, reassure them that your door is always open and they can come to you whenever they are ready. Sometimes children need more than words; they need connection. Sit beside them, hold their hand, or share quiet moments together. The goal is not to fix or advise, but to simply be there.

To deepen the moment, take turns sharing a few things, such as:

- Something that made you happy this week
- Something that felt hard or uncomfortable
- Something you wish others understood about you

This helps normalize vulnerability and reminds children that even adults make mistakes and feel deeply. End with a soft affirmation:

"No matter what happens, my love for you doesn't change."

Each conversation opens the door a little wider, showing that honesty, connection, and guidance will always have a safe place to land.

Food for Thought

After your conversation, pause for a few quiet moments to notice how it felt ~ for both you and your child. Building open communication takes patience, vulnerability, and grace, especially when honesty reveals something difficult to hear.

Remind yourself: this is growth; for you and your child. Every time they choose truth over silence, they're learning that love can hold their honesty.

Ask yourself gently:

- Did I listen more than I spoke?
- Did my tone feel safe and calm?
- Did I allow space for their feelings, even if they were uncomfortable to hear?
- How did my own childhood experiences shape the way I responded?
- What can I do next time to keep the door open even wider?

You might write a few sentences about what you learned ~ not just about your child, but about yourself. Notice the small shifts: the moments you chose understanding over reaction, softness over control. Each of these moments matters. They are how trust grows quietly, like roots beneath the surface ~ steady, unseen, and deeply strong.

WHY?

Always Explain Why

Teaching our children why we say no ~ and why rules exist ~ is really important for their safety, growth, and understanding of the world. Too often, we fall back on, *"Because I said so."* It might feel easier at the moment, but it doesn't help them understand the reason behind our rules.

When children don't know why a rule exists, they're more likely to test it out of curiosity than follow it out of respect. Giving a simple, clear explanation helps them understand the *"why,"* which builds cooperation and trust. Children are naturally curious; they want to know how things work and why things are the way they are. If they don't get answers, they might try to figure it out on their own; sometimes in ways that aren't safe.

Take the time to explain why certain behaviors could be dangerous. Instead of just saying, *"Don't run into the street,"* try:

"You might not see a car coming, and the driver might not see you. Cars move really fast, and even a few steps can be dangerous."

Better yet, show them safely ~ stand at the curb and watch cars go by, noticing how quickly they move. When we give context and show the real impact, we move from just controlling behavior to helping children learn to make safe choices on their own. This kind of guidance not only prevents accidents, it helps them think ahead and develop skills they can use in many parts of life.

Explaining rules also builds a relationship based on respect. When our children see that rules are made out of care and protection ~ not just to boss them around ~ they're more likely to follow them and understand values like responsibility and kindness. Over time, this helps them make good choices, even when adults aren't around.

You don't need long explanations for everything. Even a quick, simple reason can help your child feel respected, informed, and safe in the world around them.

Personal Reflection

When I was little, my mom told me not to put a hot glass skillet into cold water, but she never explained why. My curiosity got the best of me. I put the hot skillet in the sink and poured cold water over it. The glass cracked and exploded. Lesson learned ~ dangerous and a little funny in hindsight, but completely preventable.

This is why explanations matter.

Take the time to help your child really understand something ~ show them, explain it, use examples, or act it out. For instance, if you're teaching them about crossing the street safely, draw a simple picture to show how a parked car can block their view of oncoming traffic. Even better, go outside and practice together. Let them see how a road that seems clear can suddenly become risky.

The extra effort to show *why* helps your child make smarter, safer choices ~ not because someone told them to, but because they truly understand the reason behind the rule. That understanding is a gift they carry with them, long after the moment has passed.

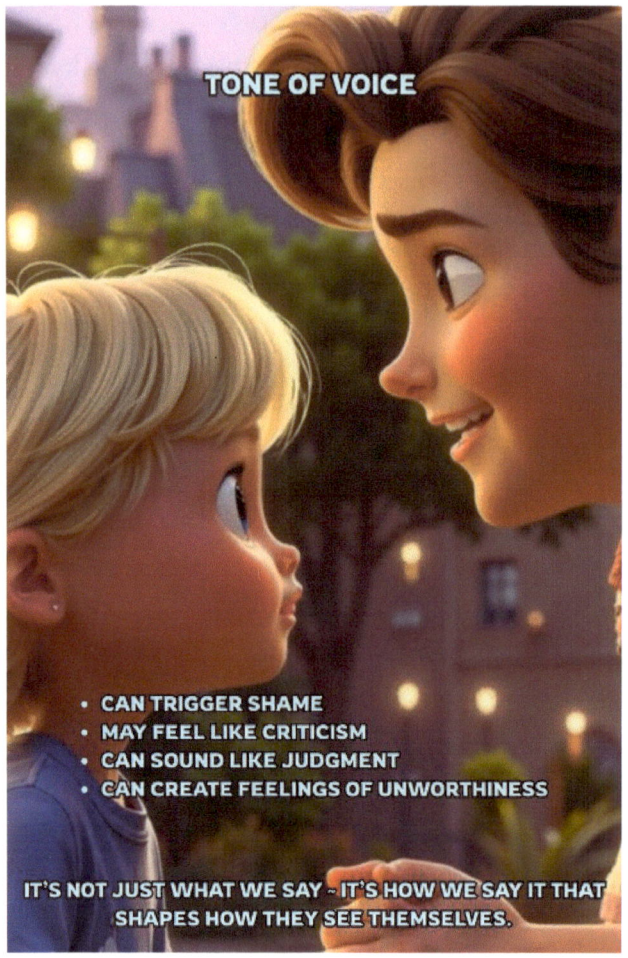

TONE OF VOICE

The tone of voice we use when speaking with our children carries as much meaning ~ sometimes more ~ than the words themselves. As adults, we often focus on what we say but may not notice how we say it. Tone conveys emotion ~ frustration, disappointment, impatience, sarcasm, or disapproval ~ even when the words themselves seem neutral. Children are incredibly sensitive to these subtle cues. A simple sentence like, *"Hurry up and get ready,"* can feel like criticism if spoken sharply, or like guidance if said calmly and gently. Sometimes, they may interpret our tone as rejection or shame, even when that was never our intention.

That's why being aware of our tone is just as important as choosing the right words. A hurried, clipped, or frustrated voice can make a child feel small or burdensome, while a calm, patient, and steady tone communicates safety, support, and love ~ even when we are correcting behavior. This doesn't mean we must sound cheerful all the time, but it does mean avoiding tones that communicate judgment or irritation. Practicing self-awareness and self-regulation is key. Taking a deep breath, pausing for a moment, or gently choosing our words and delivery allows us to express ourselves without letting frustration spill into our tone. It's not about hiding our emotions, but about expressing them in a way that invites understanding rather than fear.

Imagine asking your child to clean up their toys. Saying, *"Clean this up now!"* in a sharp, exasperated tone ~ even if the words themselves aren't harsh ~ can leave them feeling criticized, small, or unsafe. On the other hand, the same words spoken in a calm, patient, and encouraging tone can communicate the request clearly while keeping connection and trust intact. The difference isn't just in what we say; it's in **how we say it**. Tone can turn a simple instruction into a moment of learning, cooperation, and understanding ~ or it can make your child feel judged, defensive, or ashamed.

Even neutral phrases can feel very different depending on our tone. Saying, *"Nice outfit!"* with warmth and genuine enthusiasm can make a child feel seen and appreciated. The same words, said with sarcasm or a sharp edge, can make them feel criticized or embarrassed. A nagging, hurried, or dismissive tone can echo in their mind, making them feel like they're always doing something wrong. Over time, repeated exposure to negative tones can affect how they view themselves, how they respond to guidance, and how they express their own emotions.

Children notice tone everywhere ~ in instructions, corrections, or even casual comments. For example:

- *"Time for bed!"* said sharply can feel like punishment; said calmly, it becomes a simple cue for transition.

- *"Come eat dinner!"* rushed and annoyed may feel like a demand; inviting and steady, it encourages cooperation.

These small differences matter, because tone shapes how our children experience their day, how they perceive themselves, and how they connect with the adults around them.

When we speak with patience, empathy, and awareness, our children feel respected, safe, and connected. They learn to respond from trust rather than fear, and they begin to understand how to express their own feelings in ways that build understanding instead of shame. Paying attention to tone doesn't mean we have to be perfect ~ it means noticing when frustration is creeping in, taking a breath, and choosing a voice that guides rather than diminishes. Often, it's as simple as slowing down, softening our words, or showing through our voice that we are on the same team.

Next time you give an instruction or offer a comment, pause for a moment and ask yourself: *How do I sound? Could my tone be helping or hurting my child's sense of safety and self-worth?* Small adjustments in the way we speak can turn moments of tension into opportunities for learning, connection, and trust.

"Remember, children are listening not just to our words, but to the feeling behind them. Taking a moment to soften our tone can turn frustration into connection and guidance into trust."

Activity:

If you're unsure how your tone is affecting your child, try recording your conversations throughout the day using your phone or another device. Later, listen back ~ not just to the words, but to the *tone*.

Ask yourself:

- *Does my tone match the message I intended to send?*
- *Did I sound more frustrated, impatient, or dismissive than I realized in the moment?*
- *How might my child have perceived the way I spoke to them?*

Reflect on moments when your tone could have been more gentle, encouraging, or neutral. Then, as you move into the next day, be intentional about shifting your tone in similar situations.

You can even practice aloud; try saying the same phrase in different tones and listen to the emotional difference it makes. A little awareness goes a long way. By adjusting our tone, we not only become better communicators ~ we become safer, more emotionally attuned guides for our children.

Food For Thought

Remember, as a parent, we are not perfect. There will be moments when our patience runs thin, our voices rise, or we react before thinking. That's human ~ and it's okay. What matters is how we take accountability afterward. Pause, reflect, and apologize to your child if needed. Let them know gently that it was your frustration or mistake, not a reflection of them: *"I'm sorry I lost my temper just now. I was frustrated, but that wasn't fair to you, and I take responsibility for how I acted."* By doing this, we show our children that everyone makes mistakes, that taking accountability matters, and that love and connection matter more than perfection.

You've got this. Every small moment of love and attention matters.

PART II:

CHILDREN'S EMOTIONAL WELL-BEING

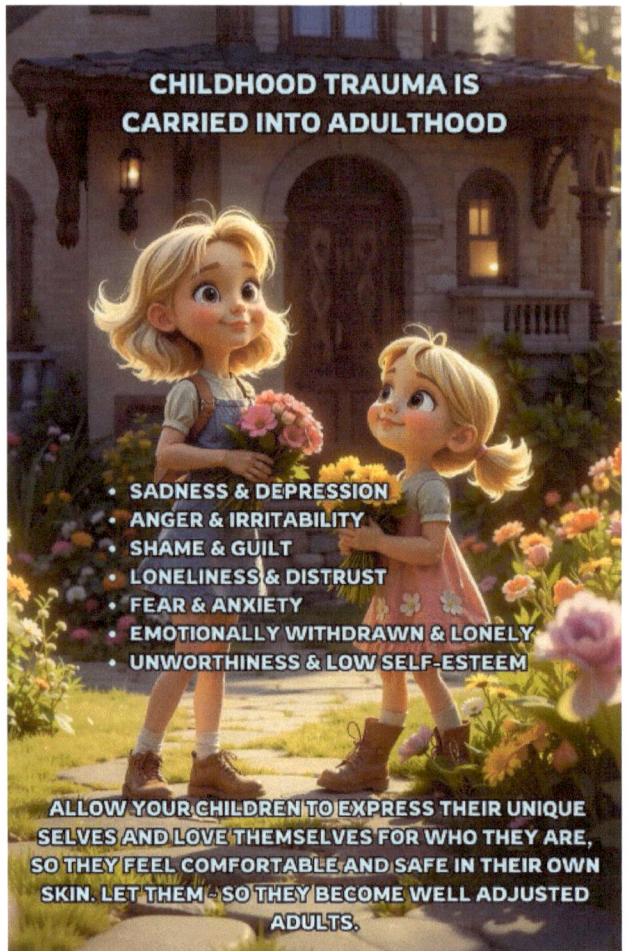

CHILDHOOD TRAUMA IS CARRIED INTO ADULTHOOD

How Childhood Shapes Us

The things our children see, hear, and feel stick with them, often long into adulthood. When they feel like they've disappointed us ~ or like they haven't become the person we hoped ~ they can carry that weight quietly in their hearts. Even when they've done their best, they may start to think their worth depends on what they achieve instead of who they are. Over time, these little moments can add up and shape the adults they become.

Childhood trauma doesn't always come from big events. Often, it slips in quietly, without anyone noticing. This isn't about blame ~ it's about being aware and choosing to create a safer, more loving environment. Sometimes it shows up in everyday moments, like these:

- **Words that hurt:** harsh criticism, sarcasm, comparisons, or labels that make a child feel "not enough."
- **Tone of voice:** sharp, nagging, or dismissive tones can stick in memory even when the words themselves seem harmless.
- **High expectations:** expecting perfection or constant achievement can make a child afraid to try.
- **Being unseen or unheard:** ignoring feelings, ideas, or achievements ~ or only noticing mistakes.
- **Favoritism:** real or perceived preferences can leave children feeling less important.
- **Too much control:** over-directing choices, discouraging independence, or stopping curiosity from growing.
- **Over- or under-protection:** keeping children from challenges or letting them face things too soon can hurt confidence.
- **Criticism disguised as teaching:** lessons that feel more like blame than guidance.
- **Lack of explanation:** not talking through rules, feelings, or decisions leaves children guessing.
- **Neglecting emotional safety:** dismissing emotions, punishing honesty, or not supporting them when they're upset.

Even small, repeated experiences like these can quietly weigh on a child. They may begin to believe they're flawed or that love must be earned. As adults, that can show up as anxiety, guilt, perfectionism, self-doubt, or trouble trusting others. Many of us build armor to protect ourselves ~ pulling back, people-pleasing, avoiding vulnerability, or hiding who we really are.

The good news? Awareness is the first step toward change. When we notice how our words, tone, expectations, and reactions affect our children, we can create a home where emotional safety comes first. That means choosing connection over control, understanding over judgment, and patience over frustration. It means celebrating effort, curiosity, and growth ~ not just results. It means showing them, every single day, that they are loved for who they are, not only for what they accomplish.

We're all learning, and none of us are perfect. We all carry our own experiences, blind spots, and the ways we were shaped. With intention, care, and reflection, we can prevent much of the unnecessary weight from forming. When children feel seen, heard, and safe, they are more likely to grow into adults who are confident, secure, and able to love and trust themselves; and others.

Childhood Awareness Checklist: Planting Seeds For Growth

Use this checklist as a guide to reflect on everyday moments with your children. The goal isn't perfection ~ it's awareness and growth.

1. Words and Communication

- Do I speak with encouragement, warmth, and curiosity more than criticism or sarcasm?
- Do I avoid labels or comparisons that make my child feel "less than"?
- Do I explain rules and expectations in ways that make sense to them?

2. Tone and Delivery

- Am I aware of how my tone shows frustration, impatience, or disapproval?
- Do I take a breath or pause when I feel my voice rising?
- Can I say the same words calmly and still get my point across?

3. Expectations and Pressure

- Are my expectations realistic and age-appropriate?
- Do I celebrate effort, curiosity, and persistence as much as results?
- Do I notice when pressure might make my child afraid to try new things?

4. Emotional Awareness

- Do I truly see and hear my child, even when it's messy or inconvenient?
- Do I acknowledge their feelings without judging or dismissing them?
- Do I show that mistakes are part of learning, not a reason to feel ashamed?

5. Independence and Choices

- Do I give my child space to make choices and learn from their own experiences?
- Do I avoid over-directing or over-protecting in ways that limit growth?
- Do I explain why rules exist rather than saying "Because I said so"?

6. Fairness and Consistency

- Do I treat all children in the household fairly, avoiding favoritism?
- Are rules and boundaries consistent and clear?
- Do I follow through calmly and predictably without anger or criticism?

7. Leading by Example

- Do I show kindness to myself and take responsibility when I make mistakes?
- Do I handle challenges with patience, curiosity, and problem-solving?
- Do I let my children see that learning and growing never stop?

8. Reflection and Growth

- Do I pause regularly to notice how my words, tone, and actions affect my child?
- Am I willing to apologize, make things right, and adjust when I slip up?
- Do I create a home where honesty, curiosity, and emotional sharing feel safe?

Activity:

Reflect and Observe

Notice how your words, tone, and actions affect your child's feelings and sense of comfort.

Steps:

1. Choose a calm moment - Pick a time when things are quiet at home, like after dinner or during a walk, so you can notice interactions without distraction.

2. Reflect for a day or two – Pay attention to:

- The words you use (instructions, corrections, praise)
- Your tone of voice (frustrated, calm, rushed, patient)

- How you respond when your child makes mistakes or asks questions
- Moments where you connect versus moments where you try to control

3. Write down your thoughts – answer a few simple questions:

- Did my tone ever sound sharp or critical?
- Did I focus more on effort than just results?
- Did my child seem hesitant, nervous, or withdrawn? Why?

4. Try one small change – pick something to do differently the next day:

- Speak one instruction calmly instead of rushing
- Praise effort at least once
- Pause before reacting when frustrated

5. Notice the difference – at the end of the day, jot down any changes you saw in your child or how you felt. This isn't about being perfect. It's about noticing patterns, practicing small changes, and building stronger connections over time.

Thank you for taking the time to do this ~ your effort shows how much you love and care for your child, and it makes a real difference in their life.

CHILDHOOD LONELINESS ~ FEELING ALONE IN THE WORLD

The Need to Belong

Every child carries a quiet need ~ to feel seen, safe, and connected. Beneath every story, every behavior, every silence, there's a longing to belong. It's one of the most basic human needs ~ to feel accepted, included, and loved for who we are.

When that need isn't met, a child can start to question their worth.

They might begin to wonder, *"Do I matter?"* or *"Do I fit in?"* Belonging is the soil where confidence and self-worth grow. Without it, they may feel uncertain about themselves or try to change just to be accepted.

As parents, we have the power to nurture belonging through the small, consistent ways we show up. By listening, noticing, and including our children in our daily moments, we communicate something sacred: *You belong here. You don't have to earn it. You already do.*

True belonging begins at home. It's built when children feel safe expressing who they are ~ when their ideas, feelings, and personality are welcomed with curiosity instead of correction. It's in those everyday moments of acceptance that they learn their voice matters, that their presence adds something special to the family.

The Hidden Feeling of Loneliness

Loneliness doesn't always look lonely. Sometimes it hides behind smiles, laughter, or independence. Children don't always say, *"I feel alone."* Instead, they might act out, pull away, or seem distant. Some children become extra helpful or cheerful, masking the ache inside because they don't want to be a burden. Others grow quiet, retreating into their rooms or their thoughts.

Every child has moments when they feel unseen or misunderstood; it's part of growing up. When that feeling stays for too long, it can begin to whisper lies: *"I don't matter."* or *"No one notices me."* That's why noticing matters so much.

Sometimes, the hidden feeling of loneliness shows up as behavior we don't expect. A child might talk back, cry easily, or seek extra attention. What looks like misbehavior is often a message: *"Do you see me?"*

Our job isn't to fix the loneliness right away, but to make space for it. To slow down, soften, and show our children that their emotions are safe with us. When they feel they can bring their sadness, fear, or loneliness without being judged or dismissed, healing begins.

When a Child Feels Alone

Even surrounded by people, a child can still feel alone. Loneliness isn't about being physically by themselves ~ it's about feeling unseen, unvalued, or misunderstood. Maybe they're struggling at school, comparing themselves to others, or feeling like they don't quite fit in. Sometimes, it's the quiet child who feels invisible, or the loud one who's really calling out to be noticed.

Loneliness can show up in many ways ~ through friendship struggles, big life changes, family tension, or simply feeling different in a world that asks them to blend in. When we notice our children feeling this way, it's natural to want to fix it right away. Sometimes, though, the most helpful thing we can do is pause and meet their feelings with empathy, creating space for them to be heard.

Instead of rushing to solutions, we can remind ourselves to truly listen. Sitting quietly beside them, asking gentle questions like, *"Can you tell me what's been making you feel this way?"* or *"What helps you feel connected?"* can open the door to understanding. We don't have to have all the answers ~ just being present often provides the greatest comfort.

When we consistently show our children that they are seen and accepted, they begin to feel their way back to connection. Saying things like, *"You are never alone. You belong with me,"* isn't about fixing loneliness ~ it's about reflecting our presence, patience, and love. Even when they are with us, they can still feel lonely if they haven't found spaces where they fit in, friends who understand them, or activities that allow them to express themselves.

Discovering what your child enjoys ~ whether it's playing guitar, drawing, sports, or another passion ~ can open a whole new world for them. Through these interests, they connect with others, express their unique selves, and build confidence, joy, and a sense of belonging from the inside out.

If you notice your child's loneliness stretching on for weeks or affecting how confident they feel, it can be a gentle nudge for you to reach out for support. Sharing connections with others ~ friends, mentors, or safe adults ~ can help them feel less alone, and reaching out yourself is part of showing how much you care.

Activity:

Noticing and Supporting Connection

Take a moment to reflect on the moments your child feels connected, and look for little ways to encourage more of them.

1. Observe for a day or two – Notice moments when your child seems joyful, engaged, or quiet and withdrawn. Pay attention to:

- When they light up talking about friends, hobbies, or interests
- Times they seem hesitant, lonely, or unsure of where they belong
- How they respond when you sit with them or ask gentle questions

2. Reflect in a journal or notebook – Consider:

- What activities or interactions bring out their joy or confidence?
- Are there moments where they seem disconnected, even when around others?
- How do I respond when they seem lonely or withdrawn?

3. Encourage self-expression – Identify one small way to help them explore their interests or passions. For example:

- Play music together, sketch, or write a short story
- Join a club or group where they can meet like-minded peers
- Simply let them show you what they enjoy and share in it

4. Create connection moments – Spend a few intentional minutes each day:

- Sit together without distractions

- Ask gentle, open-ended questions like, *"What was the best part of your day?"* or *"What do you wish more people knew about you?"*
- Listen without trying to fix things immediately; presence can be the most powerful support

5. Notice the difference – At the end of the day or week, jot down small changes:

- Did they open up more?
- Did you notice a spark of joy or confidence?
- Did this time help you feel closer?

This isn't about having all the answers or fixing everything. It's about paying attention, being there, and sharing small moments of connection. Just showing up, listening, and noticing your child ~ lets them feel that they matter and truly belong.

.

IS YOUR CHILD A PEOPLE PLEASER?

Many of us know what it feels like to walk on eggshells ~ trying not to upset anyone, doing what's expected, or keeping quiet to keep the peace. If you grew up that way, it can feel familiar when you see your child doing the same.

Sometimes children learn to please others so they can feel safe, avoid conflict, or earn love and approval. This might come from criticism, high expectations, teasing, or growing up in an environment where love feels like it has to be earned. Over time, they might start to believe they're only as good as what they do, instead of who they are.

The world often praises children who are "easy," helpful, or agreeable, which can send the message that being kind means always putting others first. While kindness is a beautiful quality, our children also need to know that their own feelings and needs matter just as much as anyone else's. When they hide who they are to keep others happy, they can start to feel unseen, drained, or unsure of themselves.

Noticing the Signs

You might notice your child:

- Says yes when they really mean no
- Apologizes often, even when they haven't done anything wrong
- Changes their opinions to fit in
- Avoids sharing their true feelings to keep everyone happy
- Feels anxious about mistakes or letting someone down
- Looks for constant reassurance or approval
- Tries to take care of everyone else's feelings

Sometimes this behavior starts as a way to feel safe or loved, but if it continues, it can lead to perfectionism or always putting others before themselves.

It can help to pause and gently reflect:

- Does my child seem to "earn" attention by doing things right?
- Do I notice myself praising them more when they behave or achieve?
- Do they seem afraid to disappoint me?
- Did I grow up feeling like I had to please others to stay safe or loved?

These questions aren't about blame ~ they're about awareness. Many of us learned these same patterns in our own childhoods. Once we see them clearly, we can make small changes that help our children learn something different.

Helping Our Children Feel Safe Being Themselves

Helping our children find their voice isn't about teaching them to argue or say no to everything. It's about showing them it's safe to be honest and have boundaries, even when it's hard.

Here are some gentle ways to do that together:

- **Listen first**

Let them share before jumping in to fix or explain. Sometimes being heard is all they need.

- **Show their feelings matter**

You might say, *"That sounds tough,"* or *"I get why that upset you."*

- **Let them see you say no**

Show that it's okay to need space, rest, or to speak up kindly.

- **Notice honesty, not perfection**

Say things like, *"I love that you shared what you really think,"* or *"That was brave of you."*

- **Love them for being, not doing**

Try to notice moments beyond grades, chores, or good behavior. Simple words like, *"I just love being with you,"* or *"You make my day better,"* remind them that your love isn't something they have to earn.

- **Be honest about your own mistakes**

When you lose patience or say something you regret, own it and apologize. It teaches them that love and connection don't disappear when we fall short.

- **Ask gentle questions**

"How did that feel for you?"
"Did you do that because you wanted to, or to make someone else happy?"

When we show our children that it's safe to be themselves ~ even when they make mistakes or disagree ~ they learn that love doesn't depend on pleasing others. They learn that they don't have to walk on eggshells to be accepted.

It's deeply important that our children grow up feeling that who they are is enough. When we do our own inner work ~ learning, healing, and staying open to growth ~ we teach them that it's okay to keep becoming. Our willingness to grow gives them permission to do the same, and that's how we build a home where truth and love lead the way, not perfection.

Activities:

1. For Parents to Reflect On

Take a few quiet minutes to think about your own experiences growing up and how they might shape the way you parent today. These reflections aren't for judgment ~ they're for understanding.

Ask yourself:

- Did I feel like love or approval had to be earned in my childhood?
- Was I afraid to make mistakes or disappoint someone?
- Do I ever catch myself expecting my child to be *"good"* instead of just being themselves?

- How can I remind my child - and myself - that love doesn't have to be proven?

Each time we pause to reflect like this, we create more room for understanding ~ for our children and for ourselves. Healing these patterns begins with awareness, and every small step we take helps both generations feel more seen, safe, and free to be who they really are.

2. Helping Your Child Feel Safe Being Themselves

Notice small ways to help your child feel free to be honest, expressive, and true to who they are.

Steps:

1. Observe

For the next day or two, notice moments when your child seems quiet, hesitant, or overly eager to please. Pay attention to what's happening around them: your tone, their body language, or what's being asked of them.

2. Reflect

Ask yourself:

- Did my child hold back an opinion or apologize quickly?
- Did I praise them more for doing something "right" than for being themselves?
- Did I give them space to say what they really felt?

3. Connect

Try one small shift today:

- Encourage them to share an honest thought, even if it's different from yours.
- Praise their effort or courage to speak up.
- Say, *"You don't have to be perfect to be loved,"* or *"I like hearing what you really think."*

4. Revisit

At the end of the day, jot down what you noticed. Did they seem more relaxed? Did you?

Thank you for taking the time to reflect on this. Your awareness and care mean more than you may ever know. Each small effort helps your child grow into someone who feels safe, confident, and loved for exactly who they are.

REJECTION

When Our Children Feel Rejected

Rejection is part of life, and our children will face it ~ just as we do. It can leave them upset, disappointed, or even doubting themselves. How we respond during these times can help them feel seen, loved, and safe, no matter what. Rejection doesn't go away completely, which is why it's so important to help our children build self-esteem early. When they feel confident in who they are, rejection won't take away from how they see themselves.

We can help our children understand that sometimes, people or situations simply aren't a good fit ~ they don't match who we are or what we truly want. That doesn't mean something is wrong with them; it just means life is redirecting them. Teaching them that the universe has a way of guiding us ~ even through disappointment ~ helps them trust that what's meant for them will find its way, often when they least expect it.

Every child will face moments when they aren't picked for a team, feel left out with friends, or experience a setback at school. These moments can leave them frustrated, sad, or wondering if they're "enough." As parents, watching our children go through rejection can be incredibly hard. It can stir up a deep ache ~ that instinct to step in, fix it, or protect them from pain. Sometimes we feel like roaring at the world or taking the hurt away ourselves. Other times, the rejection may look small from the outside ~ not making the cheerleading team, missing out on a football game, or feeling unpopular ~ but to our children, it can feel devastating. It can shake their confidence and leave a heavy weight in their hearts, and it's just as hard for us to watch.

What matters most in these moments is that we stay close. Our children don't need us to take their pain away; they need to know we're here. When we listen without rushing to fix, we show them that their feelings matter. When we hold them and let them cry, we teach them that sadness is safe to feel. When we help them name what they're feeling, we give them tools to understand it instead of burying it.

By staying calm, present, and attentive, we give them what rejection tries to take away ~ a sense of belonging and worth. Our love becomes their safety net, reminding them that even when life hurts, they are never alone.

Helping Our Children Feel Safe and Seen

The most important thing we can do when our children face rejection is to make sure they never feel rejected at home. This isn't about fixing the situation. It's about connection, understanding, and guidance. Here are some ways to walk beside them:

- **Practice Emotional Awareness Together:** Let your children see that feeling disappointed is normal and doesn't make them any less worthy. Share your own feelings in ways they can understand, so they know it's okay to feel and talk about emotions.
- **Validate Their Feelings:** Avoid brushing off their sadness or telling them not to feel a certain way. Try saying something like, *"I can see why that hurt you. It's okay to feel upset."* Showing you understand makes a big difference.
- **Offer Perspective, Gently:** Remind them that one experience doesn't define who they are. Let them know this moment is just one part of life, not the whole story.
- **Encourage Healthy Ways to Cope:** Suggest ways to work through feelings - drawing, journaling, talking to someone they trust, or taking deep breaths. Give them tools that help, not solutions that erase the hurt.
- **Celebrate Courage, Not Just Results:** Focus on the bravery it took to try, not whether they succeeded. Let them know their effort is always noticed and valued.
- **Stay Close and Connected:** Be present after tough moments. Ask questions like, *"How did that feel for you?"* or *"Was there a time you felt left out?"* Listening and paying attention shows them they are truly seen and supported.

Activity:

Reflection Questions for Parents

1. How do I usually react when my child experiences rejection? Do I rush to fix it, or do I take a moment to listen first?

2. Are there subtle signals I give - a tone of voice, a sigh, a shake of my head - that might make my child feel rejected at home?

3. Can I recall a time when I faced rejection as a child or adult? How did it feel, and what helped me move forward? Could sharing this with my child help them feel less alone?

4. Which coping strategies could I introduce or model for my child when they feel disappointed or left out?

5. How can I celebrate effort and courage in my child, even if the outcome isn't what they hoped for?

6. Am I giving myself space to grow and learn alongside my child as we face challenges together?

7. How can I show through my words, tone, and presence that my child is always seen, valued, and loved - even when things don't go as planned?

By being aware of our reactions, tone, and presence, we help our children understand that rejection doesn't diminish them. It's not a reflection of who they are or who they can be. Our love, connection, and guidance are what truly shape their sense of self-worth.

Rejection is part of life, but it doesn't define them ~ we do.

A CHILD CAN EASILY EXPERIENCE EMOTIONAL ABANDONMENT

Our children can feel emotionally abandoned more easily than we might realize ~ and it isn't because we don't care. Life's demands, stress, and the small distractions of everyday life can pull us away, sometimes without us even noticing. Emotional abandonment doesn't always look like leaving a child alone; it can happen even when we're physically present.

A child can sense when our hearts or minds aren't fully with them ~

when we're scrolling on a phone, preoccupied with work, or weighed down by stress. It shows in the little things: not making eye contact while they're talking, giving a distracted "uh-huh" or "that's nice" without truly listening, or moving on quickly instead of reflecting on what they're saying. To a child, these moments can feel like invisibility.

Sometimes words that might seem harmless to us ~ *"You're overreacting,"* *"It's not a big deal,"* or even *"Stop crying"* ~ can land deeply in a child's heart. When those words are paired with distance or distraction, children can feel dismissed, unheard, or alone. Emotional abandonment is not about intentional neglect; it's the small ways we fail to fully show up, over and over, that leave an impression.

It's worth reflecting on these patterns. Think about times in your own childhood when you felt unseen or unheard. What made you feel invisible? What moments still stick in your memory? Those experiences often surface quickly when triggered, even if many of the smaller details have faded. Recognizing these moments helps us be more mindful with our own children.

Preventing emotional abandonment doesn't require grand gestures. It begins with simple, consistent presence. Truly listening, reflecting back what they feel, and showing with our words, attention, and eye contact that we are fully present can make a profound difference. Our children notice when we pause a conversation to focus on them, respond with curiosity, or simply acknowledge: *"I see you. I hear you. You matter to me."*

Even brief experiences of emotional abandonment can leave lasting impressions. Children may feel misunderstood, invisible, or unimportant. They may want to share their thoughts and feelings but feel there's no space to do so. Left alone with difficult emotions, they can start to believe their struggles don't matter or that their voice isn't heard ~ even when they try to speak up.

The effects ripple far beyond childhood. They shape self-esteem, a sense of security, and the ability to form trusting, healthy relationships. That's why it's so important to create real emotional connection with our children. By making space for open communication, validating their feelings, and showing love consistently, we give our children the foundation to feel valued, understood, and supported as they grow.

Activities:

1. Parent Reflection: Noticing Emotional Distance

Take a few quiet moments to think about your daily interactions with your child. Ask yourself:

- When I'm physically present, am I truly listening? Or am I thinking about work, my phone, or the next thing on my to-do list?
- Do I make eye contact and respond in a way that shows I'm fully paying attention? Or do I give quick "uh-huh"s or distracted nods?
- Are there words I sometimes use that might dismiss or minimize their feelings, even unintentionally? (*"It's not a big deal," "Stop overreacting,"* or *"You're fine."*)
- How do I handle moments when I'm stressed or tired? Do I pull away emotionally, or do I make an effort to connect?

Now, reflect on a specific moment from the past week. Maybe your child tried to share something important, and you were distracted, or perhaps they were upset and you didn't fully respond. How might that have felt to them? What could you do differently next time to show them they are seen, heard, and valued?

Finally, think of a way to reconnect today ~ even for a few minutes. Sit down together without distractions, ask them about something that matters to them, or simply acknowledge how they're feeling. These little moments add up and show your child that your presence is real, consistent, and loving.

2. Daily Check-Ins

Make checking in a daily habit, even in small ways. Ask gentle, open-ended questions like:

- *"Do you feel safe today?"*

- *"Is there anything on your mind?"*
- *"Do you want to talk about something that's been bothering you?"*

These moments are invitations for your child to share what's really on their mind and in their heart. When you truly listen, give them your full attention, and respond with care, they feel seen, heard, and noticed ~ exactly as they are.

Even small gestures ~ making eye contact, pausing what you're doing, or simply acknowledging how they feel ~ tell them they matter. Let them feel, every day, that their thoughts and emotions are important, and that they are never invisible in your presence.

JEALOUSY

Jealousy in our children often comes from a deep need to feel seen, loved, and safe. From the very beginning, children look to us ~ parents, caregivers, family, friends ~ for reassurance, attention, and affirmation. They want to know, *"Do I matter? Am I enough?"*

Sometimes jealousy appears quietly. Maybe one child notices that a sibling is getting more attention after a school achievement, or feels overlooked when a parent spends extra time helping another with homework. Even small moments ~ a parent laughing a little longer at one child's joke, praising a sibling for tidying their room, or spending extra time with one child because they need more help ~ can make a child feel insecure or left out. These moments are usually unintentional, but to a child, they can feel very real.

Jealousy can also arise from comparison outside the home. At school, in sports, or among friends, children notice who gets praised, who wins recognition, or who seems more popular. When they start measuring themselves against others, even subtly, they may feel *"less than"* or question their own worth.

How jealousy shows up varies from child to child. Some express it openly; through frustration, teasing, or trying to "one-up" a sibling or peer. Others hold it quietly inside, feeling sadness, self-doubt, or hesitating to celebrate someone else's success. Even small behaviors, like clinging to toys, drawing attention to themselves, or asking, *"Why does she get more than me?"* are signs that something important is stirring inside.

Helping our children deal with jealousy starts with creating a safe space where they can be honest about their feelings. Let them know it's okay to feel jealous ~ it doesn't make them bad or selfish. When you notice jealousy, gently bring it up and ask about it: *"I see you're feeling upset; can you tell me more about what's going on?"* or *"What do you think is causing that feeling?"* Listen without judgment, acknowledge their experience, and dig a little deeper with empathy.

Sometimes, after this kind of conversation, your child may no longer feel jealous because their perspective has shifted or they realize something about the situation they hadn't noticed before. Other times, the feeling may linger. In those moments, continue to ask, reflect, and support them as they work through it. Help them identify what triggers the jealousy and come up with ways to respond ~ whether it's focusing on their own strengths, celebrating what they do have, or finding ways to connect with others rather than compare. The goal isn't to erase the feeling, but to help them understand it, name it, and manage it in a healthy way.

To help your child stop comparing themselves to others, point out the things that make them special and unique. Encourage them to notice and celebrate these things about themselves ~ not to compare, but just to see who they are. Celebrate small wins together, notice moments when they are kind, creative, or brave, and remind them of these strengths. Help them set little goals and explore what's important to them. Over time, these simple habits help children feel good about themselves from the inside, building confidence and self-worth that doesn't depend on how they match up to anyone else.

Activity:

The Strengths Tree

Steps:

1. Find a calm moment

Choose a quiet time with your child and a place where you can sit together without distractions. Gather a posterboard, paper, markers, crayons, and anything your child enjoys using.

2. Draw the tree

Together, draw a large tree on paper or poster board. This tree will represent your child and all the things that make them unique.

3. Create the leaves

Have your child draw or cut out shapes for leaves and attach them to the branches. On each leaf, encourage them to write or draw something that makes them special ~ a talent, a personal quality, a kind action, or an accomplishment. Examples could be:

- *"I'm a caring friend"*
- *"I helped my sibling today"*
- *"I'm good at drawing"*

4. Reflect gently

Look at the leaves together. If you notice comparisons, like *"I want to be as fast as my brother"* or *"I wish I could do what she does,"* guide your child back to self-recognition. Every leaf represents something only they can bring into the world. Their strengths are unique, and no one else's tree will look the same.

5. Revisit and grow the tree

Add new leaves as your child discovers strengths or celebrates achievements, big or small. If jealousy comes up, remind your child that everyone has their own tree and special leaves ~ it's okay for trees to look different. Emphasize that noticing one leaf doesn't take away from another ~ love and attention aren't limited.

Through this reflective exercise ~ and your ongoing attention and encouragement ~ you help your child see their own value, build confidence, and understand that their worth isn't dependent on comparison. They learn that joy can come from celebrating themselves, rather than measuring themselves against anyone else's journey

WHAT IS YOUR CHILD'S SELF-WORTH BASED ON?

Every child carries a quiet question in their heart: *Am I enough?* From the very beginning, they look to us ~ the people they trust most ~ for clues. The way we notice them, listen to them, and respond to their feelings helps shape how they see themselves. Their sense of worth doesn't come from grades, trophies, or what others think ~ it grows in the small, tender moments when they feel truly seen, valued, and safe.

Self-worth grows from many little experiences, but relationships are some of the strongest influences, especially the bond with us. When children feel steady love, consistent presence, and genuine understanding, they begin to feel deep down that they are enough just as they are. These relationships act like mirrors, reflecting back parts of themselves they may not yet fully see ~ their kindness, curiosity, creativity, and heart.

Feeling capable and confident matters too. When we notice effort, celebrate progress, and encourage curiosity, children start to trust themselves. Praise is most helpful when it focuses on growth, not just results. When love or praise feels conditional, children can begin to believe they have to earn it.

Friendships and connections with peers also shape a child's sense of belonging. Feeling included, appreciated, and valued ~ whether at school, on a team, or with friends ~ helps them know they matter. These experiences also teach them about themselves and what they enjoy. As they explore these relationships, it's important to give children space to make choices, try new things, and follow their interests, with our guidance nearby. This balance helps build both confidence and independence.

Outside influences ~ like media, culture, or the opinions of others ~ quietly shape how our children see themselves as well. Sometimes, the things children hear or see from people they admire can make them feel proud, but other times it can make them doubt themselves and feel like they aren't enough. Every child is different. Some naturally trust themselves, while others need gentle reminders and steady support to see their own light.

A child's self-worth grows when they feel accepted, supported, and valued for who they are ~ not just for what they do. As parents, we can help them notice and celebrate the qualities that truly matter: kindness, curiosity, creativity, empathy, courage, and heart. We can remind them, *"You are enough just as you are. I see your kindness, your curiosity, your creativity, your courage, and your big heart. You don't need to be the best or do the most to matter. True confidence comes from being yourself, enjoying what you love, and knowing that you are loved exactly as you are. Success isn't about doing the most or being the best ~ it comes from finding joy, being authentic, and trusting the goodness within you."*

Encourage your child to honor what makes them unique. Celebrate the things that light them up, make them different, and help them shine. Like snowflakes, no two are alike. These gifts are not just special ~ they become the foundation of their self-worth and well-being for life. Remind them often that being themselves is enough, and that your love and belief in them will always be steady, no matter what.

Activity:

Connection Check-In

A weekly *Connection Check-In* can help bring your child's uniqueness to life. Find a quiet moment together and ask gentle questions like:

- "What do you think makes you special?"
- "Is there something you really love about yourself?"
- "How are you feeling about where you fit in right now?"
- "Are there any struggles you're facing that you want to talk about?"
- "How can I help you feel more confident, secure, or loved this week?"
- "Is there a new activity or hobby you'd like to try?"
- "What's something fun or exciting you've been curious about lately?"

Explore their interests beside them. Take a class, try something creative, or learn a new skill together. Ask with curiosity, *"If you could try anything in the world, what would it be?"* Then listen with excitement and encouragement.

When children feel that kind of attention, love, and curiosity from us, they begin to understand a simple, life-changing truth: they are deeply valued ~ not for what they do, but for who they are. That truth, lived and felt every day, is the greatest gift we can give them.

FEAR

I still remember the way fear felt as a child ~ the racing heart when I had to stand in front of the class, the dread of walking down a dark hallway alone, the worry that I'd lose a friend if I said the wrong thing. Even small worries could feel monumental, and the unknown seemed like a trap I had no way out of. Children experience fear in very similar ways. For them, fear can feel enormous, overwhelming, and all-consuming. When they don't know what will happen, how to handle a situation, or how others will respond, they might worry they'll be abandoned, unloved, or completely alone. These emotions can leave them feeling helpless, unsure, and unprepared to face the unknown.

As parents, our instinct is often to jump in ~ soothing, fixing, or rushing to solve the problem. True emotional growth, however, comes from helping our children stay with the feeling, to notice it and move through it. Instead of rushing past fear, we can hold space for them ~ calmly, lovingly ~ while they navigate it. We can remind them that even when fear feels overwhelming, they are safe, and the feeling will pass.

It's important not to shame them if they're not ready to face their fears. Give them the time they need to process, and let them know it's okay to move at their own pace. At the same time, we can gently encourage them to take small steps forward, reminding them that we can't control the outcome. There are no guarantees, but we won't know what's possible unless we try. Balancing patience, support, and gentle encouragement helps children feel empowered rather than pressured.

Sometimes fear shows up in specific situations, like worrying about losing friends. When that happens, start by noticing and acknowledging the feeling. Let your child know that it's okay to feel that way. You might say, *"I see that you're worried about losing your friends. That makes sense ~ it's hard not knowing who will stay in your life. You don't need to change who you are to be accepted. If someone walks away because you aren't who they want you to be, that doesn't make you any less valuable. Your worth stays the same, no matter what anyone else does or thinks."*

By responding this way, you're not just comforting them in the moment ~ you're helping them practice noticing fear without being controlled by it. By sitting with fear together, noticing it, and reminding our children that they are seen, valued, and never alone, they begin to understand something powerful: fear is temporary, but their own strength is lasting. They learn that discomfort doesn't automatically mean danger, and uncertainty doesn't automatically mean disaster. This quiet understanding builds confidence, inner power, and resilience ~ gifts that stay with them for life.

Even as adults, many of us cope with fear by avoiding it ~ through busyness, unhealthy relationships, or distractions. Real courage comes from presence. Feeling fear fully, noticing it, and letting it pass allows us to reclaim our power. By teaching our children this skill, we give them one of the most profound gifts imaginable: the ability to move through life with courage, trust, and self-belief.

Activity:

1. Facing Fear Together

One way to help children build courage is to experience their fears alongside them:

- If your child is afraid of the dark, try sitting quietly in a darkened room together. Light a small candle or flashlight, talk about what feels scary, and breathe through the discomfort together.
- If they are nervous about social situations, you can role-play conversations with peers, practicing what to say or how to respond to teasing or exclusion.

The goal isn't to remove the fear but to show them they can be present with it; and that they are not alone.

Learning to stay with emotions instead of running from them opens the door to something remarkable: freedom, strength, and a deep trust in themselves.

2. Staying with the Fear

Teach your child the life-changing skill of staying with fear ~ without trying to fix it, escape it, or push it away.

- Invite them to talk about what scares them, letting them know it's okay to feel everything. Resist the urge to offer quick solutions or judgments. Simply be present. Sit with them. Hold them close. Let them feel safe while experiencing the fullness of their fear. These moments leave a lasting memory: a memory of fear felt, yet not faced alone.

- Lead by example. When you feel afraid or uneasy, don't hide behind distraction or busyness. Take a deep breath and move through it. Show that courage isn't the absence of fear; it's choosing to keep going, even when it's uncomfortable.
- Walk through difficulties together instead of avoiding them. True strength grows in these moments ~ not from pretending everything is fine, but from making space for feeling, recovering, and healing. In doing so, children learn a quiet truth: genuine joy and resilience come not from fixing every problem, but from knowing they have the strength to face whatever life brings.

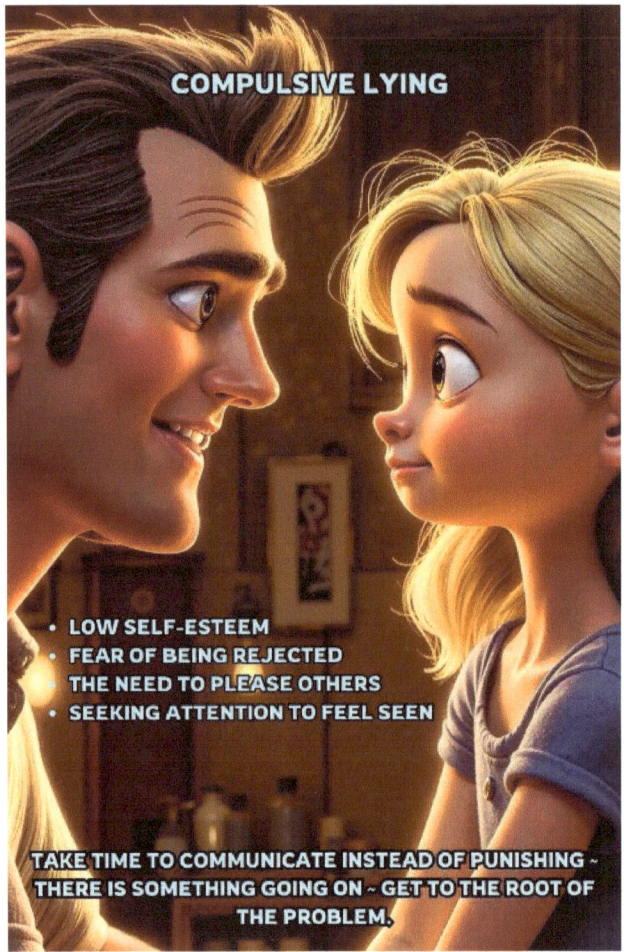

COMPULSIVE LYING

Compulsive Lying: What's Really Going On

I want to talk about something that can feel really hard for us as parents ~ when our children lie a lot. Most of the time, it's not really about the lie itself. The lie is just the surface of something deeper. Beneath it, there is often fear, worry, or a feeling that they aren't quite enough.

Sometimes they feel like nothing they do is ever enough, or like they have to be perfect to avoid trouble or criticism. Lying can start to feel like the safest way to protect themselves. It can become a shield ~ a way to escape consequences, gain approval, or hide from the disappointment they feel inside. Over time, if we don't notice it, lying can become a habit rooted in fear.

As parents, we have so much influence over how our children experience honesty. If we only point out what they do wrong, they can start to feel that their value depends on being perfect. When we notice the little things ~ their efforts, their courage, their kindness, or even their honesty when it's hard ~ they begin to understand something powerful: telling the truth is safe, and it matters.

We also want them to feel safe emotionally and physically. Part of guiding honesty is helping them understand that we love them, that we don't want them to get hurt, and that we are there to protect them while they learn. Honesty isn't just about others trusting them ~ it's about helping them trust themselves, like themselves, and feel proud of who they are.

Creating a Safe Space for Truth

Our children need to feel safe to be honest. If home feels like a place where mistakes are met with anger, shame, or disappointment, honesty becomes risky. When we respond with understanding instead, they begin to see that telling the truth doesn't put them in danger. It strengthens relationships, builds trust, and shows them they are loved for who they are. You might say, *"I know telling the truth can feel scary. I'm proud that you were honest, and we'll figure this out together."*

Truth and Consequences

Telling the truth doesn't mean there won't be consequences. When our children admit to something they did wrong, it's a chance to learn, not just a moment for punishment. Facing the natural outcomes of their actions helps them see how their choices affect others ~ and themselves. Sometimes, as parents, we feel embarrassed, frustrated, or uncomfortable, and it's tempting to sweep things under the rug or protect them from what's coming. Loving our children doesn't mean avoiding those moments. It means setting aside our own feelings and helping them navigate what happened. In doing this, we teach integrity, responsibility, and confidence, while letting them know they are safe and supported ~ even when mistakes happen.

Honesty and Friendships

When your child is struggling with a friendship, you can help them understand what's happening in a way that feels supportive. You might explain that sometimes telling the truth can make things feel complicated, and a friend might get upset or pull away. This doesn't mean *they* did anything wrong. It's a reminder that real friendships need trust, honesty, and effort from both people. When someone chooses to leave instead of talking things through, it shows more about the friendship itself than about your child's worth or actions. You can gently explain:

"Friendships take work. When someone walks away instead of working through a problem, it doesn't mean you did anything wrong. It just shows they weren't ready to respect honesty. True friends are willing to face challenges, forgive, and grow together."

Moments like this help us shift into another important lesson about honesty, one that goes beyond friendships and reaches into how our children care for themselves. These conversations remind us that honesty isn't only something we offer others; it's something that protects and strengthens them, too.

We want our children to understand that being honest helps protect themselves ~ emotionally and physically ~ from situations where hiding the truth could hurt them. This is about keeping them safe and helping them feel confident in their own decisions.

Finding the Why Behind the Lies

Lying usually points to something deeper; a fear or a need that isn't being met. You can help your child explore that safely. Create a space where honesty feels safe and they won't be judged. Ask gentle questions like, *"What makes it hard to tell the truth?"* or *"What are you worried might happen if you are honest?"* Really listen. Hear them. This is about connection, not correction.

Confidence is part of the solution too. Children who lie often crave approval or feel pressure to prove themselves. Celebrate who they are, not just what they do. Notice their effort, their creativity, their courage, and their kindness. Show them that they don't need to hide behind lies to be loved.

When children feel safe, seen, and valued, honesty flows naturally. They begin to understand that telling the truth builds trust, strengthens connections, and deepens love. They see that being themselves is always enough, and that honesty isn't risky ~ it's powerful. They also learn to protect themselves, to like themselves, and to be proud of who they are, emotionally and physically.

Activity:

Role-Play Scenarios for Practicing Honesty

Each of these scenarios can be role-played back and forth. You can switch roles so your child plays the parent and sees how honesty feels from another perspective. Afterward, you can gently reflect together on how it felt and what they learned.

1. The Broken Toy

- Scenario: Your child accidentally broke a toy or something at a friend's house.
- Prompt: *"Imagine you just noticed the toy is broken. How could you tell me the truth?"*
- Reflection Questions:
  - *"How did it feel to say what happened?"*
  - *"What worries came up?"*
- Tip: Emphasize that telling the truth helps people trust each other and keeps them safe.

2. Hurtful Words

- Scenario: They said something mean to a friend or sibling.
- Prompt: *"Your friend looks sad because of what you said. How could you tell them you're sorry and explain what you were feeling?"*
- Reflection Questions:
  - *"How did it feel to admit it?"*
  - *"What could happen when you're honest about your feelings?"*
- Tip: Show that honesty builds stronger relationships, even when it's hard.

3. Forgetting a Promise

- Scenario: They forgot to do a chore or a promise they made.
- Prompt: *"You promised to help clean up, but you didn't. How could you tell me what happened?"*
- Reflection Questions:
  - *"Was it scary to admit it?"*
  - *"How did it feel when you said it out loud?"*
- Tip: Remind them that mistakes happen, and honesty helps everyone move forward.

4. Feeling Peer Pressure

- Scenario: A friend wants them to do something they know isn't right.
- Prompt: *"Your friend is asking you to do something you're uncomfortable with. How could you tell them the truth about what you want?"*
- Reflection Questions:
  - *"Was it hard to say no?"*
  - *"How does telling the truth make you feel inside?"*
- Tip: Highlight that honesty protects them and shows self-respect.

5. Worrying About Losing a Friend

- Scenario: They fear a friend will stop liking them if they tell the truth about something.
- Prompt: *"You're worried your friend might be upset. How could you explain your side honestly?"*
- Reflection Questions:
  - *"How did it feel to share what was true?"*
  - *"What did you learn about yourself when you were honest?"*

Practicing honesty through role-play with your child will help them see that telling the truth isn't just about avoiding trouble ~ it's about building trust, showing respect, and understanding their own feelings. When they experience honesty from both sides, they learn that being truthful strengthens relationships and helps everyone feel safe and connected. Encourage them to keep practicing honesty in small, everyday moments so it becomes a natural part of who they are.

Reassure them that being truthful is about trust and that their worth doesn't depend on someone else's reaction. True friends value honesty and care about how you feel.

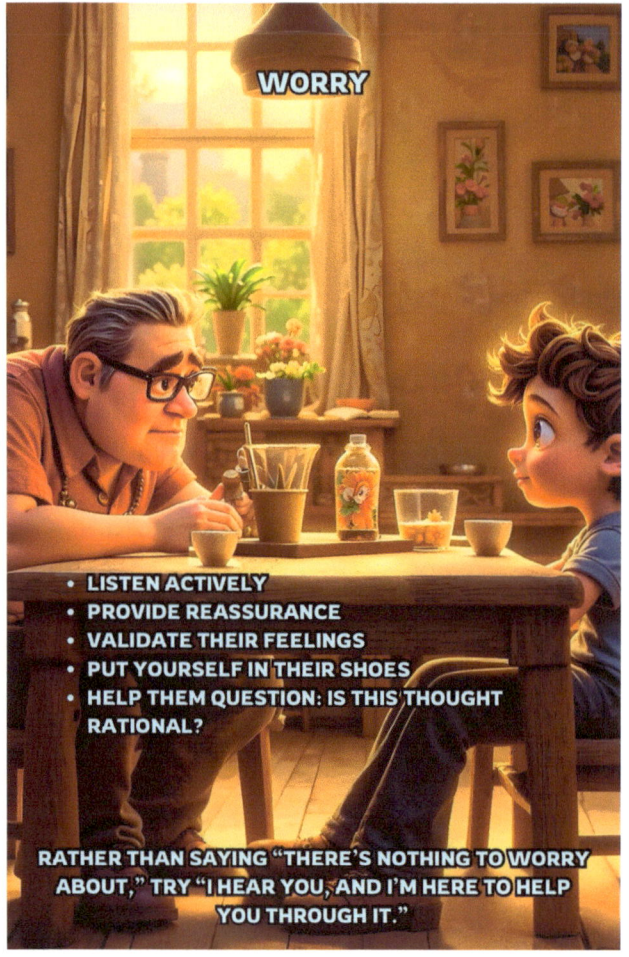

WORRY

Understanding Childhood Worry

Worry is a natural part of childhood. As our children grow and try to make sense of the world around them, their minds often fill with questions, doubts, and fears. *What if I fail? What if they don't like me? What if something bad happens?* These worries can feel big and heavy for a little heart that hasn't yet learned how to sort through them.

As parents, it's easy to want to make the worry disappear; to say,

"There's nothing to worry about," or *"You're fine."* We mean well, but those words can sometimes make a child feel unheard or alone. What they really need in those moments isn't for us to fix it; it's for us to feel it with them.

When we pause, listen deeply, and simply sit beside their worry, we teach something powerful: it's okay to feel afraid, uncertain, or overwhelmed. Even the fears that seem small or irrational to us are very real to them. The goal isn't to erase the worry, but to help them feel safe enough to face it.

It's also important to remember that children perceive the world differently than we do. What feels minor or manageable to us can seem enormous to them because they don't yet have the life experience to put things into perspective. When we respond with patience and openness instead of logic or dismissal, we show them that their inner world matters. Try to see through their eyes, not your own, and meet them where they are ~ with understanding instead of correction.

Try to step into their world for a moment. Ask gentle, open-ended questions:

- *"What's been on your mind?"*
- *" What are you most worried might happen?"*
- *"What does it feel like inside when you think about that?"*

You don't have to have all the answers. Sometimes just being there ~ quietly holding space ~ is what calms the storm. When we show empathy instead of rushing to fix, our children learn that feelings aren't something to hide or be ashamed of.

By treating their worries seriously and walking through them together, we help them build emotional strength and trust in themselves. Over time, they learn to pause and ask gentle questions that bring clarity and calm:

- *"Is this something I can control ~ or something I can let go of?"*
- *"Is this thought true, or is it my fear trying to protect me?"*
- *"What's the worst that could happen ~ and how could I handle it if it did?"*

- *"What else might be possible besides the scary thing my mind is imagining?"*

These questions help children notice when their anxiety is speaking and remind them that not every *"what if"* needs an answer; only reassurance. Teach them to replace the endless *"What if...?"* with a simple, steady *"I'll handle it."*

With practice, this becomes their inner anchor ~ helping them move from panic to peace, from uncertainty to quiet confidence.

Once the worry is out in the open, explore it together. Is it something real that can be prepared for, or a thought that just feels true because it's scary? If they're anxious about an upcoming test, help them plan and remind them of past times they succeeded. If they're afraid of monsters under the bed, start by validating their fear ~ even if you know the monsters aren't real, their feelings are. Spend time helping them feel safe: check under the bed together, add a night-light, or create a comforting bedtime ritual. You might stay on the floor nearby for a short while or show that you're not afraid, showing calm confidence they can lean on.

Then, begin introducing tools they can use when fear shows up. Together, ask gentle questions like, *"Is this something real, or is it my imagination?"* or *"What do I know is true right now?"* Encourage calming strategies like deep breathing, picturing a peaceful place, or repeating a brave phrase such as *"I'm protected and safe."* You can also help them imagine a "bravery shield" ~ a soft, glowing armor that surrounds them and keeps them safe through the night. This kind of visualization helps them feel strong and in control, turning their imagination into a source of comfort instead of fear.

Over time, your steady presence and these small tools will help them feel truly secure ~ both in your care and in their own growing courage. By continuing to take their concerns seriously, offering reassurance, and helping them learn what they can and can't control, you're nurturing their inner courage. You can gently remind your child, *"Some things are my job to worry about, not yours. You can hand that one back to me."* This helps ease their load and deepens their sense of safety, showing them that while fear is normal, they never have to face it alone.

Activity

The Worry Tree

This simple, creative activity helps children name their fears, understand them, and see how courage can grow from awareness.

What You'll Need:

- A large sheet of paper or poster board
- Markers, crayons, or colored pencils
- Sticky notes or small slips of paper

Steps:

1. Draw the Tree

Draw a big tree with roots, a trunk, and branches.

- Label the trunk: *My Worries*
- Label the left branches: *Realistic Fears*
- Label the right branches: *Unrealistic Fears*
- Label the roots: *Solutions & Strengths*

2. Name the Worries

Invite your child to share what's been bothering them. Write each worry on a sticky note and place it on the trunk. This step alone ~ acknowledging the worry ~ helps release some of its power.

3. Sort the Fears

Go through each one together and ask:

- *"Is this likely to happen?"*
- *"What makes you think so?"*

- *"Have we faced something like this before?"*
- Place the more realistic worries on one side and the imagined or exaggerated ones on the other.

4. Grow the Roots

For realistic fears, brainstorm what could help ~ studying, practicing, asking for help, or taking deep breaths. Write these as "roots," showing that problem-solving helps the tree grow stronger.

For unrealistic fears, write down comforting truths or affirmations near the roots:

- *"I am safe."*
- *"This thought doesn't have to control me."*
- *"I can take a deep breath and let it go."*

5. Decorate and Reflect

Let your child decorate the tree with colors, stickers, or drawings. When it's finished, hang it somewhere visible as a reminder that worries can be faced, sorted, and softened ~ with help and love.

The Worry Tree becomes more than a project ~ it becomes a symbol of courage and connection. It tells your child: *You're not alone with your fears. Together, we can face them, name them, and grow stronger through them.*

GRIEF

Grief and Emotional Presence

Facing the loss of a loved one, or walking alongside a child who is grieving someone in their life, can feel incredibly overwhelming. As parents, it's tempting to hide our pain, thinking that shielding them will protect them. I've been there, trying to appear *"strong"* while my heart was heavy, worrying that my kids would be frightened by my tears. I've learned that showing our real feelings, even when it's messy, is one of the most powerful lessons we can give.

Letting your child witness your emotions doesn't harm them. It teaches them that life can be hard, feelings can be big, and strength isn't the absence of sadness. Strength is moving through those feelings ~ with courage, honesty, and support. When children see us cry, struggle, and still move forward, they learn that sensitivity and courage can exist side by side. They see that being fully human is something to honor, not hide.

Creating a space for grief is about **presence more than perfection**. Your child doesn't need you to have all the answers or to *"fix"* the pain; they need you to be there. Encourage conversation by gently asking:

- *"What are you feeling right now?"*
- *"What part of this is the hardest for you?"*
- *"Is there a memory you want to share about them?"*
- *"What do you wish you could say?"*

These questions invite reflection and give words to feelings that can feel overwhelming. Even quiet children benefit from your calm presence ~ sometimes simply sitting together in silence or holding them through tears communicates more than words ever could.

Grief can be confusing. Children may wonder why the person is gone, why life feels different, or why emotions feel so big. Help them name their feelings ~ sadness, anger, guilt, or confusion. Validate them, letting them know it's okay to feel however they feel. Avoid phrases like, *"Don't cry"* or *"They're gone, get over it."* Instead, try:

"It's okay to feel this way. I'm here with you. We'll get through this together."

It's also important to show healthy coping. Let your child see you acknowledge your grief. Share your memories, your tears, and even the ways you process sadness. Show that it's okay to ask for help, to take time, and to lean on others. Sometimes professional support ~ a counselor or mentor ~ can help, and there's no shame in reaching out.

Help your child understand that grief looks different for everyone, and it may change from day to day. Some moments will feel heavy;

others lighter. Encourage small acts to honor the person who is gone: sharing a story, drawing a picture, or lighting a candle. Even brief rituals can give a sense of connection and comfort.

Activities:

Explore Grief Together

1. Memory Box

Create a Memory Box with your child to hold memories of the person who has passed.

What You'll Need:

- A small box or container
- Paper, photos, or small objects that remind you of them
- Pens, markers, or stickers for decorating

Steps:

1. Invite your child to decorate the box however they like.
2. Encourage them to write notes, draw pictures, or place meaningful objects inside.
3. Share your own memories and add items too.
4. Revisit the box together whenever they want to remember, talk, or reflect.

This activity gives children a way to remember someone and share their feelings in their own way.

2. Sharing Stories Together

Sometimes grief isn't about a "big moment" ~ it's the small, everyday memories that keep someone alive in our hearts.

Steps:

1. Set aside 10–15 minutes to share a story about the person you lost.
2. Encourage your child to tell a favorite memory, funny moment, or something they wish they could say.
3. Share your own memory as well.
4. Reflect together: *"How does it feel to remember this?"* or *"What does this memory remind you of?"*

This practice helps children see that it's okay to talk about their feelings ~ whether sadness, love, or happiness ~ and sharing this way naturally brings you closer.

Food for Thought

Grief doesn't follow a timeline, and every child experiences it differently. By sitting with them through their feelings and exploring them together, you give them a gift ~ a sense of safety, the understanding that they are seen, and the ability to recognize and talk about their emotions.

Just being there, patient and loving, shows your child it's okay to feel deeply and that they are never alone in their sadness. You can gently remind them: *"Being open about your feelings isn't a weakness ~ it's a kind of strength. Healing doesn't come from pretending life is easy. It comes from love, connection, and the courage to face whatever your heart is carrying."* Through these shared moments, children learn that vulnerability and strength can live together, and that it's okay to be fully human.

CRYING

Crying Isn't Weakness: Teaching Children to Feel Fully

One of the most powerful lessons we can give our children is that crying ~ and allowing themselves to really feel their emotions ~ isn't a weakness. It's an act of courage. Too often, children (and adults!) grow up thinking tears are something to hide, a sign of weakness, or that they shouldn't feel so much. Emotions aren't something to push aside or ignore ~ they're part of being human. When we let ourselves feel, cry, and be honest about what's inside, we learn more about ourselves, grow, and heal.

Facing our feelings actually takes more courage than avoiding them. Crying is strength. Vulnerability is bravery. Pretending to be "tough" or holding back tears may look like strength, but it isn't. When we allow ourselves to feel deeply, share our emotions openly, and show our children that it's okay to do the same, we teach them that true strength isn't about never crying ~ it's about being honest with yourself, embracing what you feel, and moving through life with heart. Meeting our children's tears with empathy instead of discomfort gives them the freedom to be fully human.

Sharing Feelings Together

Being there when your child is upset is one of the easiest and most powerful ways to help them understand their feelings. Sit with them, hold their hand, or put a gentle hand on their shoulder, and let them talk or just be quiet. You can ask simple questions to help them notice what's going on inside, like:

- *"What made you feel sad?"*
- *"Which part feels the hardest?"*
- *"What would help you feel a little better?"*

We can also share our own feelings in age-appropriate ways. I've found this so powerful with my own children. They know the real me ~ messy, imperfect, and human. They know I've made mistakes, done things I regret, and struggled with myself. They see who I am today: striving to grow, learning every day, and moving forward. Sharing this doesn't burden them ~ it shows them that change is possible and that even the hard feelings can be faced and understood.

When children see our vulnerability, they learn that all emotions are valid. Struggles, regrets, and challenges don't make someone unworthy of love ~ they're just part of life. That openness encourages them to share their own feelings, knowing they'll be met with acceptance rather than judgment.

As your child starts to feel safe sharing their feelings, you can offer simple ways to support them ~ taking slow, deep breaths together, quietly drawing how they feel, or just noticing what's happening inside. The goal isn't to stop the tears or "fix" the feelings, but to sit with them, support them, and show that their emotions are real and okay. Being present this way teaches our children that it's safe to feel, to share, and to handle big emotions.

Activity:

Sitting with Tears

This simple moment helps your child feel safe with their emotions and reminds them that crying isn't something to hide ~ it's something human.

What You'll Need:

- A quiet, comfortable spot
- A blanket or cozy corner
- Your calm, loving presence

Steps:

1. Create a calm space

Find somewhere soft and peaceful - maybe a cozy corner with pillows or a blanket. Let your child know, *"It's okay to cry here. All your feelings are welcome."*

2. Acknowledge what you see

If your child is crying, stay close and gentle. You might say, *"I can see you're really sad right now. It's okay to feel that way. I'm right here."* Sometimes just being there means more than any words.

3. Show them it's safe to feel

You can show openness by sharing a little of your own heart:
"I get sad sometimes too. When I do, I like to sit quietly until I feel ready to talk."
This helps them see that everyone has big feelings - even grown-ups.

4. Breathe together

Take slow, deep breaths side by side. Maybe put your hand on your heart and invite them to do the same. "Let's take a few calm breaths together." Breathing helps the body settle when emotions feel big.

5. Talk gently when they're ready

When the moment feels right, you might ask:

- *"Can you tell me what's been making you feel sad?"*
- *"What do you think could help you feel a little bit better?"*

Keep your tone soft and patient. Sometimes they won't have words yet - that's okay too.

6. Offer comfort.

A hug, holding their hand, or just sitting quietly together can help more than anything you say. It's about helping them feel *safe while they feel*.

7. Express together.

If they want, suggest drawing, journaling, or building something small that shows what their feelings look like.
For example:

- *"Want to draw what your sadness looks like?"*

- *"Would you like to make a little heart out of clay to keep with you when you feel this way again?"*

These quiet moments teach that tears aren't a problem to fix ~ they're part of being real, and part of healing.

Food for Thought

Avoid shaming your child for crying. Tears are part of how we all learn, release, and heal. Labels like "crybaby" may seem small at the moment, but they can quietly shape a child's self-esteem and make them afraid to share their feelings. Instead, pause, take a deep breath, and remember: they're not trying to upset you ~ they're doing their best to communicate. Your calm presence shows them that emotions are welcome and that you're a safe place to land.

Caring for our children in the midst of tears can be challenging. Sometimes we get frustrated, triggered, or lose our patience ~ and that's okay. These moments are opportunities to learn more about ourselves and our children. If you need to step back, breathe, or apologize afterward, do it. Showing your child that you can recognize your own reactions, make amends, and reconnect teaches them something powerful: everyone makes mistakes, and love and understanding can always be restored.

When your child shares their feelings, respond with patience and attention. Help them find words for what they feel, and celebrate the effort: *"Thank you for sharing your feelings with me. That takes courage."*

Don't hide your own emotions. Let your children see you notice, feel, work through, and express what's inside. They'll learn that all emotions ~ joy, sadness, fear, frustration, and everything in between ~ are natural, and none need to be hidden. By showing your feelings openly, you show your children that you're human, not perfect, and that parenting doesn't mean pretending everything is always okay. Life is real, messy, and full of challenges; and that's what makes it meaningful.

Embracing your own emotions teaches your children that it's safe to be authentic, take up space with their feelings, and move through life honestly. Emotional growth isn't about perfection; it's about showing up, being present, and being consistent. By doing this, you give your child one of the greatest gifts: the courage to feel fully, the confidence that they're safe, and the knowledge that love remains steady even when emotions run deep. You show them that life can be lived with heart, openness, and real strength ~ and that being human is the most powerful form of courage there is.

SELF-HARM

As parents, some questions can shake us to our very core:

Why would my child want to hurt themselves?

Why would they choose to cut or stop eating?

What am I missing?

What did I do wrong?

These questions are heavy. They come with a storm of fear, guilt, confusion, and heartbreak. In the middle of that storm, it's important to remember one thing: our children aren't trying to hurt us ~ they're trying to survive a pain that feels too big to carry alone.

Self-harm isn't about seeking attention or being dramatic. It's a silent cry for relief ~ a way to release feelings that feel unbearable. For some children, it's a way to feel a small sense of control in a world that feels completely out of control. When they hurt themselves, they decide when and how it happens. It becomes something they can manage when everything else feels impossible. Restricting food, or other forms of self-denial, can do the same ~ it gives them a false sense of power when their world feels unsteady.

These behaviors aren't "bad choices." They're signs of deep emotional pain; the only way some children have learned to cope. Beneath those actions are feelings that run heavy: fear, grief, anxiety, shame, self-blame, and a deep sense of not being enough. Sometimes they can't find the words for what they feel, so they turn those feelings inward, toward their own body.

That pain doesn't come from nowhere. It grows from the spaces where our children feel unseen, unheard, or unaccepted. Criticism, teasing, comparison, or emotional distance can quietly plant seeds of shame. Even when we are struggling ~ with stress, loss, or our own pain ~ they can mistake that distance as proof that they don't matter.

Outside the home, the pressures don't stop. Bullying, exclusion, and the constant comparison of social media can make them feel like they'll never measure up. The message they absorb becomes: *"I'm not enough. I don't belong. Something is wrong with me."*

Even loving adults ~ teachers, coaches, and relatives ~ can add to the weight without meaning to. High expectations, pressure to perform, or trying to shape them into something they're not ready to be can quietly make them question their worth. What our children really need is to know they're allowed to be who they are ~ not who the world expects them to be. They don't have to be perfect; they just need to feel loved for exactly who they are.

When Your Child Is Hurting

The most powerful thing you can do for a child who is hurting themselves is to simply be there. Sit beside them. Hold them if they'll let you. Let them feel what they're carrying ~ without trying to fix it, explain it away, or rush it.

Self-harm is often a way to cope when feelings feel too heavy to bear. It can be an escape, a way to manage grief, anger, shame, or fear when they don't know how else to cope. Healing doesn't come from taking away the behavior alone; it comes from helping the feelings underneath rise safely and be understood. Children need to know it's okay to feel deeply. Tears, grief, shame, anger, fear ~ none of these are too much. None of these make them unworthy of love. They need to learn that they can face these feelings without something terrible happening.

Understanding this helps us shift into what matters most as parents: showing up. You don't need all the answers. You don't need to know exactly what to say or how to fix it. What matters most is that you stay. Your calm, patient presence says more than words ever could: "I see you. I'm with you. You're not alone."

Children who turn to self-harm are often carrying pain they don't know how to name. Many of them don't feel seen or accepted in other parts of their world. Sometimes this begins at home without anyone realizing it; other times it starts at school, with friends, or in social circles where they feel different or misunderstood. That sense of "I don't belong anywhere" can make their inner world feel too big and too heavy to hold.

This is where we come in. We help them slow down and sit with the feelings they've been trying so hard to outrun. We gently guide them to notice what's happening inside and to put words to the pain they've been carrying. When those feelings are finally allowed to surface ~ without judgment, without fear ~ they can begin to release. Healing begins in these quiet moments of honesty, where a child feels safe enough to tell the truth about their inner world.

Communication, shared feelings, and unconditional support are the foundation. These are the places where real healing can start. Professional help, mentors, and trusted helpers can also play an important role. What matters most is that your child doesn't feel alone in the dark.

Supporting a child through self-harm is one of the hardest paths a parent can walk. It will test your patience, your strength, and sometimes even your hope. You may feel scared, overwhelmed, or unsure. You might react in ways you wish you hadn't. That's okay. What matters is that you keep showing up ~ that you apologize when needed, that you listen, and that you remind your child they are seen, valued, and deeply loved.

Being a parent in these moments doesn't mean being perfect; it means being real. It means embracing the messy, painful, beautiful reality of life together. When you keep showing up with love, courage, and presence ~ even when you're tired or afraid ~ you give your child one of the greatest gifts imaginable: the deep knowing that they are safe, that they are worthy, and that they are never, ever alone.

Activity:

The Safety Circle

This activity creates a place where your child can be real with their feelings, even the heavy ones, and know they're safe with you.

What You'll Need:

- A soft blanket, candle, or something comforting that feels special
- A calm, private space where you both feel at ease

Steps:

1. Create the Space: Sit together somewhere peaceful ~ maybe on the bed, the couch, or a corner filled with pillows. Lay out your blanket or light your candle. Let your child know this is your *Safety Circle* ~ a space where all feelings are welcome.

2. Set the Intention: Say something simple like, *"In this space, we can talk about anything. There's no judgment, no rush, just love."*

3. Invite Sharing: Ask gentle questions when your child is ready:

- *"What's been feeling heavy lately?"*
- *"What would help you feel a little lighter right now?"*
- *"Would you like to talk, or just sit together for a bit?"*

4. Offer Comfort: Let the space be about presence, not fixing. You might hold hands, sit quietly, or breathe together. If words aren't ready, that's okay. Silence can still be healing.

5. End with Connection: When you're done, remind them: *"No matter what happens, this space is always here for you. We can always come back to it."*

Over time, your Safety Circle becomes a symbol of trust ~ a place where feelings can exist without fear, where love is steady, and where your child learns that even pain can be met with gentleness and care.

Parent Reflection

Take a quiet moment for yourself.

Close your eyes, breathe slowly, and think about a time in your life when you felt misunderstood, afraid, or alone. What did you need most at that moment? Maybe it was someone to simply stay beside you ~ not to !x or explain, but to listen, to see you, to make you feel less alone.

That same kind of presence is what your child needs now. You don't have to have the right words. You don't need to know how to make it all better. What matters most is that you *stay*.

Let your presence say, *"You're safe with me. You don't have to face this by yourself."*

Some days, staying calm will feel impossible. You might cry, feel angry, or lose hope for a moment ~ that's okay. Take care of yourself too. You're walking through something incredibly hard, and your love is already doing more than you realize. Healing begins not in perfect answers, but in connection ~ one quiet, honest moment at a time.

POWERLESSNESS

When our children feel powerless, it leaves a mark. It's more than not being heard ~ it's the quiet, heavy feeling that nothing they do changes anything. Their choices seem to have no weight. Their thoughts feel ignored. Life can start to feel like it's happening *to* them instead of *with* them. That sense of having no control can quietly shape how they see themselves and the world around them.

Sometimes, we unintentionally contribute to that feeling. When we decide every detail for them ~ what they wear, who they spend time with, what they do ~ children can get the message: *I'm not trusted to make my own choices.* Slowly, they may begin to doubt their own instincts, opinions, and ideas. That feeling of powerlessness can grow into a painful whisper: *I'm not enough. I can't make a difference.*

Powerlessness can show itself in different ways. Some children stop trying, convinced it won't matter. Others push themselves to impossible standards, hoping that doing everything "right" will finally give them a sense of control. Some may try to take back control in ways that worry us, like acting out, self-harm, or restrictive eating. These behaviors aren't signs of a "bad" child. They're ways of coping when life feels overwhelming and out of reach.

The heart of powerlessness is the loss of choice and influence. When children feel they have no say, they also start to doubt themselves. They need to know their ideas matter, that their feelings are valid, and that even small choices can give them real power in their lives.

What our children are really asking for is simple: *I matter. My voice matters. I have a place in my own life.*

Creating Space for Choice and Confidence

Empowerment begins quietly ~ in the moments when children are allowed to explore, make choices, and discover their own voice. It doesn't come from perfect parenting or tightly following a plan. It grows in the everyday rhythms of life: *when we slow down enough to listen, when we make room for their ideas, and when we show them that what they think and feel truly matters.*

Sometimes empowerment looks like something simple ~ pausing to notice what excites them, asking what they think, or offering a choice in small things like which game to play or how to spend a free afternoon. These tiny invitations say, *"You have a say here. Your ideas shape this moment."* Each time we step back and really listen, we reinforce that their voice has weight in their world.

When we celebrate effort rather than perfection, we give them a different message: that curiosity matters, trying matters, and mistakes are part of learning, not signs of failure. Children begin to trust themselves when they realize they don't have to get everything right to be valued. They learn they are capable of problem-solving, experimenting, and beginning again.

The way we show up ~ more than any single technique ~ is what teaches children confidence. Walking beside them with presence, patience, and openness shows them what resilience looks like. When they see us handle uncertainty with honesty and courage, they learn that strength isn't about never stumbling; it's about taking the next step with a steady heart.

Empowering our children isn't something we do to them. It's something we build with them ~ moment by moment, choice by choice ~ in ways that remind them: *Your thoughts matter. Your choices matter. You have the power to shape your own life.*

Activity:

Walking Alongside: Letting Them Lead

This activity gives your child space to make choices, explore ideas, and feel capable ~ while you stay close, supporting them without taking over. It's about connection, trust, and showing them their voice matters.

What You'll Need:

- A little time together
- An open heart
- Willingness to step back

Steps:

1. Invite their ideas. Ask your child to think of a few things they might like to do - a snack, a game, a project, or a short activity. Encourage them to choose what to do and take the lead in planning and putting it into action. Younger children may need guidance to break it down into steps, and that's okay.

2. Listen with curiosity. Ask gentle questions about what they're thinking and why. You might say, *"I love how you thought of that! Can you tell me more about it?"* or *"Which part sounds most fun to you?"*

3. Step back and stay present. Let them try things their way, even if it gets messy or doesn't go perfectly. Your calm presence shows them you trust their choices and that making decisions is safe.

4. Notice and celebrate effort. Pay attention to what they learned, what felt exciting, or how they handled challenges. Say things like, *"I loved seeing how you figured that out,"* or *"You had such creative ideas today."* Focus on courage and effort, not just results.

5. Reflect together. Afterward, talk about how it felt for them to lead and for you to follow. Share what you noticed about their creativity, problem-solving, or confidence. Invite them to notice it too.

Over time, these small moments become a quiet practice of empowerment. Children begin to see that their choices matter, that they have influence over their own life, and that they can trust themselves to make decisions. Walking alongside them this way nurtures confidence, independence, and a strong sense of being capable and valued.

ACTING OUT

Acting Out: "See Me. Hear Me. I Have Things to Say!"

Sometimes our children act out in ways that leave us frustrated, scared, or unsure. Those behaviors aren't about being "bad" or trying to push our buttons. More often, they are a way of saying something they don't have the words for: *Notice me. Hear me. I have things inside I don't know how to share.*

When a child's voice isn't truly heard ~ whether because of family stress, busy schedules, or unintentional dismissal ~ their feelings don't disappear. Anger, defiance, withdrawal, or disruptive behavior can surface instead. Trauma, bullying, or feeling powerless can make it even harder for them to express what's happening inside. Outbursts are usually a signal that something heavy needs attention. They are cries for understanding, not misbehavior.

Noticing Our Role

As parents, it's easy to react first and reflect later. Pausing to notice our own tone, words, and actions can make a big difference. Sometimes a rushed schedule, a sigh, or the words "calm down" can unintentionally dismiss a child's feelings. Brushing off their frustration or correcting every little mistake reinforces the idea that their voice doesn't matter. When we notice this, we can choose to slow down, listen, and show patience. This helps children feel truly seen.

Walking With Them, Not Fixing Them

Acting out gives us a window into the feelings, fears, and frustrations our children carry. Walking alongside them instead of trying to fix everything shows them that their feelings and choices matter. Children learn best when they see that their voice matters, that their needs are recognized, and that they are safe expressing themselves.

Balancing this with steady boundaries ~ bedtime, safety, responsibilities ~ helps them feel guided, not controlled. Flexibility matters too. Adjusting how we approach a rule or expectation shows that their individuality is valued, even while core expectations remain steady. For example, if homework is a struggle in the evening, the rule that it gets done stays. How it happens can change: sitting together, breaking it into smaller steps, or taking small breaks to focus. The expectation remains, but the approach meets them where they are.

When they notice how we respond and make small changes along the way, we show our children what it means to stay calm, patient, and kind ~ even when things feel hard. They start to see that their feelings are safe with us, that they matter, and that they can always come to us just as they are. Every one of these moments helps them grow a little stronger on the inside. It builds trust, courage, and closeness ~ the kind that carries them through whatever life brings.

There will be times when our children don't need words or explanations. Just holding them in silence or sitting together quietly can communicate love, safety, and understanding. Being present through the messy, big feelings teaches them that all emotions are welcome. These silent moments speak volumes. They remind our children that love isn't lost when things get hard, and that all feelings are welcome. Every time we choose to walk beside them instead of trying to "fix" them, we help them build trust in themselves, confidence in their voice, and a sense of belonging that follows them into every relationship and challenge ahead.

Activity:

Listening Through the Outburst

This little activity is about helping your child feel heard when big feelings take over ~ and helping you stay calm and close while you move through it together.

What You'll Need:

- A quiet space or cozy corner
- Your presence and attention
- Patience and steady breathing

Steps:

1. Set the scene. Notice when an outburst begins. Take a deep breath and remind yourself: your child isn't trying to upset you; they're carrying something heavy.

2. Create a safe spot. Invite your child to a nearby space where you can both feel calm. Let them know you're there and ready to listen when they're ready.

3. Acknowledge, don't judge. Name what you see: *"I see you're upset. I hear your frustration. It's okay to feel this way."* Avoid correcting or immediately solving the problem.

4. Ask gentle questions - if they're ready. Try prompts like:

- *"Can you tell me what's going on?"*
- *"What part of this feels hardest?"*
- *"What would help you feel a little better right now?"*

~ If they aren't ready to talk, sitting together or holding them in silence is enough.

5. Show that feelings are normal. Share a small piece about your own emotions: *"I'm feeling a bit frustrated too. I'm taking a breath, and I'm here with you."*

6. Offer connection. Sometimes words aren't needed. Being present, holding hands, or sitting quietly together communicates love and safety without speaking.

7. Check in later. After the moment passes, ask gently how they feel and what they need. Remind them: *"Even when you feel upset, I see you, I hear you, and I love you."*

After this activity, take a moment to notice how it felt for both of you. Even small moments of presence can make a big difference.

These moments are more than just managing an outburst. They're chances to walk with your child, notice what's happening inside them, and show that their voice matters.

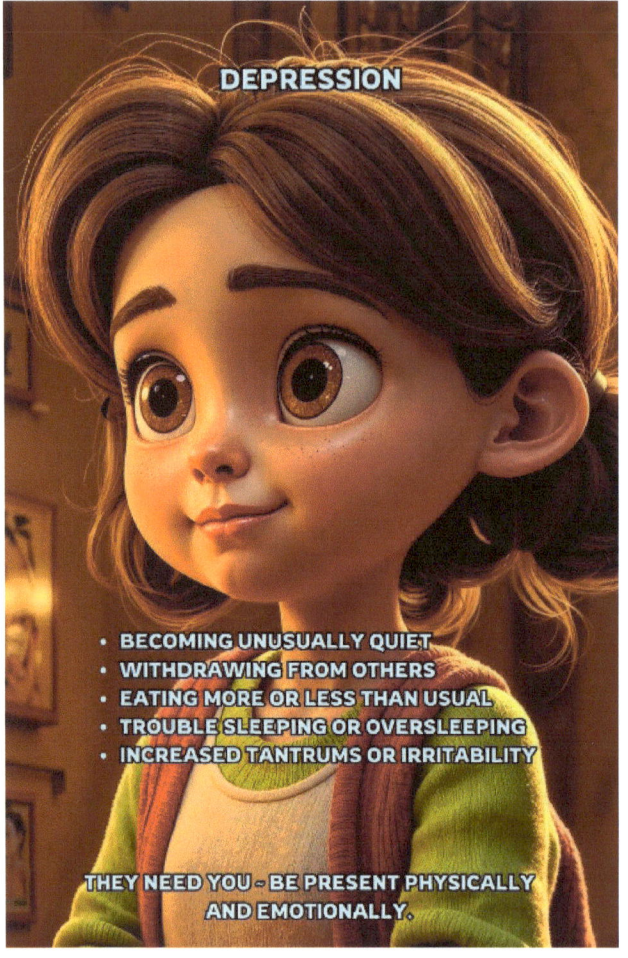

DEPRESSION

Depression in Young Children

Depression in young children can look very different from how it shows up in teens or adults. Most children don't yet have the words or self-awareness to say, *"I feel sad,"* or *"Something's wrong."* Instead, their pain shows through changes in mood, behavior, or even their body. What might seem like "attitude," "laziness," or "acting out" is often a quiet signal that something deeper is going on.

One of the most common signs is irritability or anger. A child who feels low may get frustrated easily, snap over small things, or seem more moody than usual. These reactions are not about being defiant ~ they are often signs of hurt they don't yet have words for. They may not know how to name their sadness, but their body and behavior are trying to express it for them.

You might also notice changes in play. Play is how our children process their world. When it shifts ~ becoming withdrawn, repetitive, or focused on darker themes like loss or danger ~ it may reflect how they're feeling inside. A child who once played with energy and imagination might start to isolate or go through the motions without joy.

Sometimes the clues show up physically. Frequent stomachaches, headaches, or other vague pains without a medical cause can be linked to emotional distress. You may also see changes in sleep or appetite; either too much or too little. These shifts are ways the body expresses emotional pain when words aren't enough.

Depression and anxiety often appear together. A child may seem constantly worried, tense, or fearful, expecting something bad to happen. They might withdraw socially, avoid friends or family, or lose interest in the things that once made them happy. You may notice phrases like, *"I don't care,"* or *"It doesn't matter,"* said with a kind of quiet distance.

Sometimes these moments are easy to miss, but noticing them can make a big difference. Awareness isn't just seeing the signs ~ it's also letting your child know you see *them*, that you notice something is hard, and that you care. You can gently check in: ask if they want to talk, or if there's a way you can help. Even a quiet, *"I see you, and I'm here for you,"* can mean the world.

Taking it a step further means knowing when we need extra support. Sometimes our love and attention aren't enough to help our child navigate the depth of depression or anxiety. Reaching out to a counselor, therapist, or trusted mentor shows them that their struggles are important, that they are worthy of help, and that we are willing to do whatever it takes to keep them safe and supported. They may resist at first, but deep down, they feel comforted knowing they can count on us, that someone is holding space for them, and that they are worthy of noticing and care.

What matters most is that awareness leads to action. Seeing their suffering, acknowledging it, and taking steps ~ whether through listening, supporting, or connecting them to help ~ communicates to your child that they are not alone, that their feelings matter, and that healing is possible. This mindful presence sets the stage for the next step: exploring together and building tools for coping, confidence, and connection.

Activity:

Observing Subtle Signs

This activity is a way to notice the little changes in your child ~ in their mood, energy, or behavior ~ and create space for them to share what's really going on.

What You'll Need:

- A quiet, comfortable space
- Your full attention
- Patience and presence

Steps:

1. Take a few days to observe your child's patterns - their play, energy, appetite, sleep, and tone. Notice small changes without judgment.

2. When you sense something's off, gently check in:

"I noticed you've been quieter lately. How are you feeling?"
"You haven't been playing with your friends much this week. Is something on your mind?"

3. Offer presence before advice. Sometimes just sitting together or holding them quietly says more than words can.

4. Encourage expression through creative outlets - drawing, music, storytelling, or imaginative play often reveal what words can't.

5. Validate their feelings:

"I hear that you're feeling frustrated and tired. I get it.."

6. Keep checking in over time. Let them know their emotions are safe and important, and that you'll always listen.

Taking time to notice and respond with care helps our children feel seen and understood. It builds quiet trust ~ the kind that helps them open up when life feels heavy. These small moments of awareness can make a lasting difference, teaching them that no feeling is too big or too small to share.

Food for Thought

Sometimes when we begin to notice sadness in our children, it brings back memories of our own. I didn't realize until much later that I was probably depressed as a child. I just knew I felt unhappy most of the time.

I remember how my little sister's happiness used to make me angry. I loved her deeply, but her joy made me feel jealous. I wanted her to feel what I felt, not to hurt her, but so I wouldn't be alone in my sadness. Looking back now, I see that was my way of surviving. I didn't understand what was happening inside me, and I didn't have the words for it.

Realizing that helped me see my own children differently. When they act out or pull away, I try to look for what's underneath instead of reacting right away. It reminds me how powerful it is for a child to be met with understanding instead of shame.

Sometimes our children's pain touches the same tender places we've carried for years. In those moments, we have the chance to heal together ~ to give them what we once needed: someone to stay close, to listen, and to love us through it.

ANXIETY

Understanding Anxiety in Young Children

Anxiety can start showing up much earlier than we often notice; even in toddlers. I know this firsthand because I was that anxious child. My worry and fear were always there, twisting quietly inside me. I didn't have the words to explain it, and I didn't understand what I was feeling. My parents weren't aware of the signs ~ they didn't see the tension, frustration, or quiet withdrawal ~ so I often felt alone. I didn't know what it was, only that I wanted to feel happy and safe, and I didn't.

Young children show anxiety in subtle ways. They might cling more than usual, shy away from new people or experiences, or seek comfort in familiar objects ~ a favorite blanket, stuffed animal, or pacifier ~ when facing something unfamiliar. These items are more than "just things." They provide a sense of safety and security that they may not yet be able to find in the world around them; or even from the adults in their lives. They are constant companions, always available, offering reassurance when everything else feels uncertain. When these items are lost or left behind, a child's anxiety can spike, because the object represents a calm they can't yet create on their own.

It's not a reflection of poor parenting that our children rely on these anchors. Often, we simply aren't aware of how deeply they need them, or how early anxiety can appear. By noticing and honoring these signs, we begin to understand what our children need most: a sense of safety, presence, and reassurance ~ both in the world around them and within themselves.

Anxiety can also occur alongside depression. Children who feel lonely, disconnected, or unsure of where they belong may worry constantly, imagine worst-case scenarios, or feel like they have no one to turn to. That worry can spiral into frustration, anger, or withdrawal ~ and sometimes surface through behaviors we don't immediately recognize as anxiety. This might look like restlessness, trouble concentrating, repetitive movements or routines that help them feel safe, irritability, clinginess, sudden fears, or shutting down emotionally. Some children may avoid school or social situations, hesitate to try new things, or seek constant reassurance that everything is okay. These behaviors aren't defiance or "overreacting"; they're signals of internal distress that need understanding, not judgment. When we know what anxiety can look like on the surface, it becomes easier to recognize what a child is trying to communicate underneath.

I know this because I've been that anxious child. I didn't always understand my feelings, and my parents didn't recognize the signs. Now, as a parent and caregiver, I notice the same signals in children around me. It reminds me how essential it is to truly see, hear, and support them through their anxiety, even when the signs are subtle or easy to misinterpret.

Recognizing Anxiety

Anxiety looks different in every child. Some become clingy or overly cautious. Others cry, act out, or withdraw completely. Physical signs ~ stomachaches, headaches, frequent bathroom accidents, or even bedwetting ~ often appear alongside emotional signals. Anxiety can show up as irritability, frustration, sudden bursts of anger, fatigue, or difficulty focusing.

Triggers vary. For some children, anxiety comes from a genetic predisposition. For others, it's tied to a life transition ~ starting daycare, moving, or a shift in family dynamics. Parental stress, past experiences that felt unsafe, or even small changes in routine can leave a big impact. Because children are still learning to process the world, what may seem minor to adults can feel overwhelming to them.

Anxiety can also occur alongside depression. Children who feel lonely, disconnected, or unsure of where they belong may worry constantly, imagine worst-case scenarios, or feel like they have no one to turn to. That worry can spiral into frustration, anger, or withdrawal; and sometimes manifest as behaviors that feel confusing or concerning to adults.

I know this because I've been that anxious child. I didn't always understand my feelings, and my parents didn't recognize the signs. Now, as a parent and caregiver, I notice the same signals in children around me. It reminds me just how important it is to truly see, hear, and support them through their anxiety, even when it doesn't always look obvious.

What We Can Do

Our most powerful tool as parents is presence. Just being there ~ calm, attentive, patient ~ can make a world of difference. Children are incredibly perceptive. I know this from my own experience: I felt everything my parents didn't see. Children notice tone of voice, body language, and the energy in a room long before they can explain their feelings.

Pay attention to patterns in behavior and emotion. Notice when a child avoids activities, clings too tightly, expresses physical symptoms of worry, or has sudden shifts in mood. These are not random; they are messages asking for support, reassurance, and understanding.

It's important to create a safe and predictable environment. Daily routines help children feel secure, especially when their inner world feels chaotic. Consistent reassurance lets them know it's okay to feel nervous or scared. You might say: *"I see this is hard right now. I'm here with you. We'll face it together."*

Gradual exposure to fears, gently and consistently, helps children learn that scary things aren't as overwhelming as they imagine. Walk beside them, celebrate courage, not just outcomes, and model calm, intentional behavior. Over time, they begin to trust themselves, feel more confident, and discover their own strengths.

Activity:

Helping Children Through Anxiety

A simple way to help your child feel safe, seen, and supported during anxious moments.

What You'll Need:

- A quiet, comfortable space
- Your full attention
- Patience and steady breathing

Steps:

1. Pause and Center: When you notice anxious behavior, take a breath and remind yourself: *They are not trying to upset me; they are carrying something heavy inside.*

2. Create a Safe Space: Invite your child to sit with you. Let them know you are present and ready to listen.

3. Acknowledge Emotions: Name what you see: *"I see that you're worried. It's okay to feel scared."* Avoid judgment or rushing to fix it.

4. Ask Gentle Questions: Encourage expression without interrogation:

"Can you tell me what's worrying you?"
"What part of this feels the hardest?"
"What would help you feel a little better right now?"

5. Model Calm: Share your feelings briefly if appropriate: *"I'm a little worried too, and I'm taking a deep breath. I'm here with you."*

6. Offer Connection: Sometimes presence is enough. Sit together, hold hands, or share a quiet space. Physical reassurance can communicate love and safety.

7. Follow Up: After the moment passes, check in gently. Ask how they feel now and what they might need. Reinforce: *"Even when you feel worried, I see you, I hear you, and I love you."*

Extra Tip:

- **Children are always listening and watching.** Even before they have words, they pick up on tone, body language, and energy. Anxiety is not misbehavior; it's a signal.
- **Notice patterns.** Small shifts ~ avoiding new situations, clinging, resisting activities, or sudden irritability ~ are messages. They're not random.
- **Comfort objects are vital.** Blankets, stuffed animals, or pacifiers provide safety that children can carry everywhere.

They are anchors when adults may not realize the need for reassurance.

- **Presence is the greatest tool.** Staying calm, emotionally available, and patient teaches children their feelings are safe and valid.
- **Gentle exposure builds resilience.** Walk beside your child as they face fears, celebrate effort, and model coping. Over time, confidence grows.
- **Trust your instincts.** If anxiety persists or intensifies, a child therapist or counselor can provide guidance. You don't have to navigate it alone.

OVERWHELMED

Children can feel overwhelmed for so many reasons, often in ways we might not notice. A rushed morning, a raised voice, a small change in routine, or even unspoken tension can make their world feel unpredictable and stressful. What seems minor to us ~ a different caregiver for the day, a change in plans, or a new activity ~ can feel huge to them. I've seen it happen: a normally confident child can suddenly break into tears or clinginess when the security they rely on feels shaken.

They notice everything. Our moods, worries, even the tone of our voice before we say a word can shape how they feel. That's why creating emotional safety matters. How we speak, how we guide their day, and how we stay calm and present all influence how children experience their world.

Sometimes our children don't have the words to explain what's going on inside. Overwhelm shows up in behavior:

- **Irritability or mood swings:** They get upset over small frustrations or lash out unexpectedly.
- **Withdrawal:** Spending a lot of time alone, hiding in their room, or avoiding people can be a sign of stress.
- **Crying spells or meltdowns:** Tears and outbursts may be their only way to communicate feeling out of control.
- **Clinginess:** Wanting to be near you all the time or needing lots of hugs and reassurance can mean they don't feel safe.
- **Physical symptoms:** Headaches, stomachaches, or sudden complaints of feeling sick often accompany stress.
- **Sleep or appetite changes:** Trouble sleeping, oversleeping, or disrupted eating patterns can all be clues.
- **Regressive behaviors:** Doing things they had outgrown, like sucking their thumb, wetting the bed, or acting younger than their age, can show they feel upset or unsettled.

These behaviors are not failures or acting out. They are moments for us to pause, notice, and create space for our children to feel safe and supported. They are asking, in their own way: *"I need help processing this. Please see me. Please be here with me."*

Even small changes in mood or behavior can tell us something important. Learning to notice these signs early and respond calmly helps our children feel understood and teaches them that big emotions are normal and manageable.

Activity:

Supporting Your Child Through Overwhelm

This activity is about paying attention to how your child feels, giving them a safe space to calm down, and helping them learn ways to handle big emotions.

What You'll Need:

- A quiet, safe space
- Your full attention and presence
- Patience and calm

Steps:

1. Create Predictable Routines: Morning rituals, mealtimes, and bedtime routines give children a sense of safety. Knowing what's coming next helps reduce stress.

2. Create a Calm-Down Space: A cozy corner with pillows, soft lighting, books, or a favorite stuffed animal can become their "go-to" spot when emotions feel too big.

3. Practice Deep Breathing Together: Inhale through your nose, expand your belly, then exhale slowly through your mouth. Doing it together teaches calm presence.

4. Mindful Movement or Play: Jumping, dancing, swinging, or stretching can release tension and help children feel grounded.

5. Role-Play Scenarios: Practice moments that might overwhelm them and show calm ways to respond. Demonstrate asking for help, taking a break, or expressing emotions safely.

6. Encourage Emotional Expression: Use emotion charts - or journaling for older children. Naming feelings helps them understand and manage them.

7. Praise Positive Coping: Notice positive steps. Pay attention when your child expresses their feelings in a helpful way. You could say, *"You told me you were frustrated instead of yelling ~ that was really strong of you."*

8. Cut Down on Stress Where Possible: Keep an eye on too many activities, not enough sleep, or pressure from friends or school. Make sure your child has free time to rest and relax ~ it's just as important as staying healthy.

These small practices help children feel safe and understood. They learn that big emotions are normal, that they can handle them, and that you are there to support them. The consistent presence, guidance, and tools you provide now help them feel more confident, calm, and capable as challenges come up in the future.

HATRED

Understanding Hate and What It's Really Trying to Say

Sometimes hate shows up in our children in ways that catch us off guard ~ a slammed door, harsh words, or that quiet shutdown that says, *"I don't even care."* Yet underneath it all, most of the time, they do care. Hate can come from a place you might not expect ; it can grow out of love. When a child cares deeply about someone, the pain of feeling rejected, unseen, or hurt can twist into anger, frustration, or even hatred. If they didn't care, they wouldn't feel anything at all.

Hate can be a shadow of love ~ love that was hurt, ignored, or misunderstood. When children begin to understand this, they start to see that strong feelings aren't "bad" or "wrong." They're messages from the heart ~ signals that something inside needs attention, compassion, and care.

When our children feel that kind of heavy emotion, it's easy for us as parents to react. We want to stop it, correct it, or tell them it's wrong. Hate isn't something to punish; it's something to unpack. The real work is helping them slow down enough to notice what's underneath it. Maybe they felt left out. Maybe they felt unheard. Maybe they just didn't know how to handle the hurt.

Hate is heavy to carry. It drains a child's energy; and ours too. When we hold onto it, it takes over how we see people and situations. It steals our peace, our clarity, and our joy. The longer we carry it, the more it closes the heart off from connection, and that's the opposite of what any of us really want.

Our job isn't to fix the feeling, but to guide our children back to what's real ~ to help them see that hate doesn't make them "bad," it just means something deeper inside them is asking to be understood. We can sit beside them in those moments, not with a lecture, but with curiosity.

- *What happened?*
- *What did you feel when that happened?*
- *What did it remind you of?*

Sometimes just being listened to helps them find the softer emotion underneath ~ hurt, sadness, disappointment ~ and that's where healing begins.

Letting go of hate doesn't happen overnight. Each time your child learns to name what's behind it, they take a step toward understanding themselves better. They begin to realize they have a choice ~ they can respond instead of react.

As adults, our role is to help them navigate these complex emotions with patience and presence. Hate isn't simple ~ it can come from fear, rejection, jealousy, or even love that's been broken or ignored. Emotions are rarely just one thing; they're layered, messy, and deeply human. When we help our children untangle those layers, they start to under-stand themselves ~ and others ~ more clearly.

When we help our children sort through those layers, they start to understand not only themselves but others as well. They begin to see that difficult feelings have roots, and that those roots can be explored, cared for, and healed.

They begin to notice how holding on to anger or hate affects their bodies and hearts ~ the tension, heaviness, and distance it creates ~ they start to understand the cost of carrying those emotions. That awareness opens the door to something gentler. They begin to recognize the relief that comes from choosing caring, patience, understanding, and respon-sibility for their own feelings.

These moments become powerful teachable experiences. They are not lessons we offer once; they are truths we model over and over. Every time we talk about hurt instead of hiding it, every time we pause instead of react, every time we choose connection over resentment, we show our children what it means to live with an open, steady heart.

Through consistent guidance, children learn that difficult emotions are inevitable, yet not unmanageable. They discover that feelings do not have to take control or define who they are. Releasing the weight of hate ~ step by step, with practice and support ~ becomes one of the most freeing acts of emotional strength they will ever learn.

Activities:

These activities are a way to help children see what they're feeling and practice letting go of anger or hurt safely. It shows them that big feelings are normal, that they don't have to carry them alone, and that there are gentle ways to cope. Doing it together also gives you both a chance to stay connected, calm, and present while working through the messy stuff.

You can try these approaches:

1. Talk about how hate can come from love. Sometimes a child feels hurt or angry because they care deeply about someone or something. Let them know that their feelings are meaningful, not something to hide or feel bad about.

2. Show the cost of holding onto anger. Holding onto hate or anger can make them feel anxious, sad, or tense. Explain that letting go doesn't make them weak - it actually takes courage.

3. Encourage understanding. Ask them to think about why someone might act hurtfully. When children see that others may be hurting too, it helps them respond with kindness instead of more anger.

4. Teach forgiveness. Forgiving doesn't mean what happened was okay. It means letting go of the weight of it so their heart feels lighter and calmer.

5. Practice calming techniques together. Take deep breaths, count to ten, or step away for a quiet moment. Doing this together shows them how to handle strong emotions safely.

6. Give safe ways to express feelings. Drawing, journaling, playing music, or talking with a trusted adult lets them get their feelings out without hurting themselves or others.

7. Set healthy boundaries. Let them know it's okay to step away from someone or something that's harmful. They can ask for space, speak up calmly, or remove themselves when needed.

8. Help them bounce back. Life has ups and downs. Help them take a step back, say kind things to themselves, and keep going instead of holding onto anger.

9. Show how to handle conflict. Listening, respecting others' points of view, and looking for solutions teaches our children that disagreements don't have to divide people ~ they can help relationships grow.

Remind them that hatred is never the answer. It's a signal that something deeper is going on. When we guide our children to notice this, we teach them to choose care, courage, and understanding. Choosing love over hate isn't weakness ~ it's real strength.

Food for Thought

Sometimes helping our children work through their hate becomes a mirror for us too. It reminds us of the places in our own hearts that still carry hurt, resentment, or disappointment. In guiding them toward forgiveness and understanding, we often find our own small steps toward healing too.

HOLDING THINGS IN

The Importance of Expressing Feelings in the Moment

There is something powerful about saying how we feel when we feel it. It's not always easy, but it's one of the healthiest things we can teach our children and ourselves. When emotions stay tucked away, they don't disappear. They quietly build up until one day they spill out in ways that surprise everyone; sometimes even us.

For children, unspoken feelings can feel heavy. They might not have the words yet, so they hold it all in ~ the hurt, the worry, the anger ~ until it shows up as tears, silence, or behavior that seems "out of the blue." What's really happening is that something inside has been waiting to be seen.

Holding feelings in often comes from fear ~ the fear that if we speak our truth, people won't like us, won't love us, or will leave. I know this personally. I've always been outspoken, but when it comes to people I care about, I've often held back. I worried that if I spoke up, they wouldn't be there for me or might abandon me. I tried to stay silent, to be who they wanted me to be, to accept things I couldn't truly accept. I thought I could handle it, that I could keep the peace; but inside, the pressure built like a time bomb. Eventually, it exploded, and suddenly I was labeled "too much" or "overreacting." They never saw it coming.

Our children feel this too. When they hold back their feelings to be liked, loved, or accepted, it can build to a breaking point. What looks like an outburst may actually be them finally asserting themselves after trying too hard to stay quiet. These moments are less about misbehavior and more about finally being heard after trying to survive in silence.

Talking about feelings as they come, helps them begin to understand themselves and see how their emotions affect others. It clears the air before confusion or resentment builds and opens their eyes to honesty, trust, and emotional safety ~ a place where hearts can breathe.

Holding feelings in doesn't just affect emotions; it can affect the body too. Headaches, stomachaches, restless nights, or constant tension are often signs of emotions being bottled up. You might notice your child withdrawing, becoming quieter than usual, or seeming on edge. Sometimes the ones who always say, "I'm fine," are carrying the heaviest load. They may snap at small frustrations, avoid eye contact, or go out of their way to keep peace. These behaviors are their way of managing emotions they don't yet know how to express, a quiet signal asking for understanding, patience, and space to be themselves.

Once we notice how our children carry their feelings, the next step is finding ways to help them express and understand those emotions safely.

Activity:

Helping Your Child Express Emotions

Connection is the first step. When children feel accepted, seen, and truly listened to, their hearts begin to trust that it's safe to speak.

1. Normalize emotions: Remind your child that every feeling - anger, sadness, fear, joy - is part of being human. No emotion is "bad." Every feeling is asking to be understood.

2. Teach feeling words: Help them name what's happening inside:

- *"I feel frustrated because..."*
- *"I feel nervous when..."*
- The more words they have, the easier it becomes to share.

3. The Feelings Jar:

- Create it together: Find a jar and decorate it. Label it "Feelings Jar." Keep slips of paper nearby.
- Daily check-in: Invite your child to write or draw how they felt that day.
  - *"I felt proud when I finished my project."*
  - *"I felt sad when my friend didn't want to play."*
- Sharing time: Choose a quiet moment to read a few notes together. Let your child decide whether to share or just have you listen.
- Talk and reflect: If hard emotions come up, don't rush to fix them. Listen, validate, and gently explore together:
  - *"What helped you feel a little better today?"*
  - *"What could we try next time this happens?"*

Over time, this practice helps children realize that feelings are safe to express, that they don't have to hold everything inside, and that their voice matters.

By teaching our children to speak from the heart in the moment, we give them a lifelong gift ~ the freedom to feel, to express, and to remain connected to who they truly are. They learn that being authentic is more important than being liked. They learn that love doesn't depend on silence or perfection.

If your child does "lose it" at some point, remember ~ often it's the result of holding in so much for so long, trying to be liked, trying to be loved, trying to keep everyone happy. What looks like an outburst may actually be their first chance to stand in their truth; just as I learned in my own life.

SHUT DOWN

As parents, we want the best for our children. Most of the time, we're trying our hardest, yet even with good intentions, we sometimes do things that unintentionally hurt them. It might be a raised voice, a sharp tone, an eye roll, or a sigh that carries frustration. Sometimes it's glancing at our phones instead of really listening, interrupting before they finish, or brushing off what they're feeling when we're tired or overwhelmed.

These small moments can create big feelings inside a child. What seems small to us can feel like a big disconnection ~ a break in the safety and closeness they deeply depend on. When that happens often, they may begin to pause before sharing, wonder if their feelings matter, or pull back to protect themselves. Over time, these experiences can quietly teach a child to hide their emotions, silence their needs, or try to manage everything on their own.

There are times when our children close themselves off or go quiet, and it can leave us feeling unsure of what to do. It's easy to see this as defiance or stubbornness, yet most of the time, it's something much deeper. A child who shuts down is often feeling unsafe showing what's really inside. They may be overwhelmed, embarrassed, or unsure how to express their feelings in a way that feels safe.

Understanding this changes how we respond. When we see the shut-down not as rejection, but as protection, we can meet it with patience instead of frustration. Our calm, steady presence tells them they don't have to face their feelings alone ~ we will stay close, even in the quiet.

I've found that when my child shuts down, slowing down first helps more than rushing for answers. Just being there ~ sitting nearby, reading together, or holding hands ~ says, *"I see you. I'm here."* Sometimes I share a little about my own day or how I felt in a similar moment, just to show that feelings are normal and nothing to hide. Inviting them to open up can be as simple as noticing small things: *"I saw you seemed frustrated after dinner. Do you want to tell me about it?"*

If they shake their head or stay quiet, I don't push. Staying connected in small, calm ways helps remind them that love doesn't depend on words. When they're ready, expression often returns naturally. Sometimes it shows up through drawing, journaling, or imaginative play ~ gentle outlets that give their feelings a voice until they're ready to speak them aloud. Over time, these moments of safety often lead to gentle openings ~ a few quiet words, a question, or a story that begins to unfold.

Replacing judgment with curiosity is key. Instead of asking, *"Why are you acting like that?"* try, *"Can you help me understand what you're feeling?"* Those words say, *"I want to know. I'm on your side. I won't make you wrong for feeling this way."* This approach invites understanding instead of defense and helps children feel seen, even when they don't have the right words yet.

Consistency matters. When our children know how we'll respond when feelings get big, they learn they can trust us. Calm, steady reactions help them feel safe to share what's inside. When our responses feel unpredictable ~ calm one moment and reactive the next ~ they often stay silent to protect themselves.

Words and labels can shape how safe they feel to open up. Calling a child "too sensitive," "dramatic," or "babyish" can make them believe their emotions are wrong, teaching them to hide what's real. Over time, these moments can build quiet walls inside. Emotional shutdown becomes a kind of shield ~ protection from judgment, disappointment, or misunderstanding.

When this happens, children may pull away or isolate, not because they want distance, but because it feels safer than the risk of being misunderstood. What they need most in those moments is gentleness, patience, and proof that it's still safe to be seen.

Even quiet moments can carry messages. Children notice everything ~ our tone, our energy, and our silence. They may feel invisible when their feelings go unnoticed. Our reactions ~ yelling, showing frustration, or even looking stressed ~ can make them hesitate to share. They notice that expressing themselves might upset us, so they tuck their feelings away. This isn't misbehavior or defiance; it's self-protection, sometimes even protection of us.

The good news is that we can always start again. Every moment of connection ~ no matter how small ~ helps rebuild safety. Think back to when you were little. Remember the times you felt misunderstood or scared to speak up. What did you need then? Chances are, it wasn't perfect. It was someone who slowed down, listened, and stayed near even when you didn't have the words.

That's what our children need too. Creating a space where they feel safe to show what's really going on inside ~ without fear of being dismissed, judged, or corrected ~ changes everything. When children feel seen, heard, and accepted, even quiet moments ~ a shared smile, a tear, a whispered *"I love you"* ~ become building blocks for connection. They learn their emotions are safe, real, and worthy of care. They learn that love can hold space for all of who they are.

Activities:

1. Reflection to Pause and Connect:

Take a moment to notice:

- When does my child seem to shut down most?
- What feelings might be underneath the silence?
- How do I usually respond in those moments?
- What small action could I try to show calm, presence, and patience?
- Thinking back to my own childhood, what helped me feel safe to share my feelings?

Take a few quiet minutes to write, or simply sit with these questions. Seeing these patterns and noticing our own reactions is the first step toward creating a space where our children can feel safe, understood, and loved for exactly who they are.

2. Helping Your Child Open Up

This activity is about creating a safe space for your child to share what's inside and strengthening the connection between you.

What You'll Need:

- A quiet, calm space
- Your full attention
- Patience and an open heart

Steps:

1. Start small. Ask your child to share a feeling or moment from their day. You could say, *"I noticed you seemed upset after school. Do you want to tell me about it?"* Even small openings matter.

2. Listen closely. Just be there and hear them out. Nodding, maintaining eye contact, and responding with short phrases like, *"I hear you,"* or *"That sounds hard."* Avoid jumping in to fix it.

3. Show you get it. Say back what you notice: *"It makes sense that you'd feel frustrated when that happened."* This shows them their emotions matter and you're really paying attention.

4. Offer different ways to express. If talking feels hard - try drawing, journaling, or acting it out with toys. Let them know it's okay to share in the way that works best for them.

5. Share gently. Give a small example from your own life: *"I felt nervous too when I had to do something new. Talking about it helped me feel better. What do you think might help you?"* Showing your own feelings helps them feel safer to express theirs.

6. Respond with curiosity, not judgment. Ask, *"Can you share with me what that felt like?"* rather than asking, *"Why did you do that?"* This encourages honesty and keeps the door open.

7. Stay steady. Respond the same way each time. Knowing you're consistent makes it safer for them to open up.

8. Show love. Remind them: *"I love you, no matter what. Your feelings are safe with me."*

Practicing these steps help you and your child handle big emotions now and later. They learn that their feelings are real, safe to share, and that you're someone they can always turn to. These moments build trust, closeness, and confidence that stay with them well into adulthood.

ABANDONMENT

When a Child Feels Left Behind

Have you ever seen your child go quiet after something upsetting and felt worried, confused, or frustrated? That silence can be puzzling, but most of the time it comes from a very common fear: the fear of being left behind. Children notice everything, even things we might think are small. Abandonment wounds can come from big events ~ a parent who isn't emotionally available, divorce, the death of a loved one, or the sudden loss of a friend or caregiver. They can also come from the little moments we often overlook: being interrupted, dismissed, or not truly heard. To a child, these moments can feel like the world is slipping away, leaving them wondering if the connections they care about will last. That quiet fear follows them, shaping how they relate to others and the world around them.

This fear often whispers questions they can't quite put into words: *"Am I enough? Will someone stay?"* You might notice it in clinginess, withdrawal, anxiety, emotional outbursts, or attempts to control their surroundings. Some children pull back, becoming quiet and hesitant to share their feelings. Others may seek constant reassurance or test boundaries to see if love is reliable. These behaviors aren't about being "difficult" or seeking attention. They are your child's heart trying to protect itself from hurt ~ from feeling unseen, unvalued, or abandoned.

As parents, it's natural to feel frustrated, worried, or unsure when we see these reactions. We might sigh, raise our voice, or struggle to know what to say. Many of us remember moments from our own childhood when we felt left behind, unseen, or unsure if love would last. Those memories can surface when we watch our children struggle, but they can also be our guide. Recognizing these patterns in ourselves and our children helps us respond with patience and empathy rather than judgment. It gives us the chance to turn moments of fear and withdrawal into opportunities for connection, reassurance, and trust.

Understanding the depth behind these reactions is the first step to helping your child feel safe, seen, and valued. Feeling left behind doesn't mean a child is unlovable. It means they are asking ~ quietly, sometimes without words ~ to be noticed, held, and understood. Recognizing that fear doesn't mean you failed; it means you have the chance to be the steady presence your child needs to heal, grow, and learn to trust again.

Signs Your Child May Be Struggling with Abandonment

You might notice some of these patterns in your child:

- Clinging or separation anxiety
- Trouble trusting others or making friends

- Emotional outbursts or sensitivity to rejection
- Acting overly independent to avoid disappointment
- Constantly seeking reassurance
- Nightmares, anxiety, or sadness
- Testing others by pushing them away

Some children keep it all inside, believing they're unlovable. Others try to control their world, hoping to protect themselves from more loss. Left unrecognized, these patterns can follow them into adulthood, making relationships feel uncertain or unsafe.

When Our Wounds Come Into Play

Children notice everything. They can feel our sadness, tension, or old hurts through the way we act, the tone of our voice, or even our body language, even when we don't say a word. If we've experienced abandonment ourselves, our children can pick up on those feelings and carry some of the same worries.

Some children respond by trying to take care of us, holding feelings that aren't theirs to carry. Others become anxious, watchful, or shut down emotionally, worried that if something happens to us, they will be left alone. Owning our own story without passing it on is one of the most powerful gifts we can give them.

Showing them it's safe to feel, to grieve, and to hurt makes a difference. At the same time, showing that healing is possible helps them see a path forward. Let them see you move through pain, care for your heart, and find moments of joy again. Let them witness perseverance, self-worth, and quiet strength.

Teach them this truth: just because someone leaves does not mean everyone will. People come and go for many reasons. That doesn't reflect our value. Some connections are meant to last a lifetime. Others show up to teach or guide us for a season, and that is okay.

Meeting abandonment with courage and self-compassion shows our children how to do the same. Let them see joy in friendships, creativity, laughter, and community. Remind them that love is not limited. They can love bravely, trust deeply, and rise again after loss.

Children learn more from what we live than from what we say. Let them see this truth in action:

Being left does not make you unlovable.

Your worth is not measured by who stays or goes.

You are, and always have been, enough.

When children see these truths in action, they start to feel safe and trust that we are there for them. Staying calm, steady, and consistent helps them feel secure. Once they feel that safety, we can take small steps to help them open up and feel supported.

How We Can Help Them Feel Safe Again

When a child carries the fear of being left behind, what they need most isn't perfection ~ it's presence. They look for steady signs that love won't disappear when they cry, make mistakes, or pull away. Trust is rebuilt through small, consistent gestures ~ the quiet check-ins, the soft tone, the way we stay when they expect us to leave.

How we show up every day matters more than we usually realize. The way we talk, how patient we are, and the calm we bring all send messages to our kids. When we rush their feelings or shrug them off, we can accidentally make them worry that love might not last. Showing up with understanding and steady presence says something different: *You're safe. I'm here. I'm not going anywhere.*

No one gets it right all the time, and that's okay. What really matters is how we come back after a tough moment ~ saying sorry if we lose our patience, reconnecting, showing them that mistakes don't break love. Over time, seeing us return again and again helps them understand that love sticks around, even when things get messy.

Activity:

The Quiet Bridge

Create a calm space where your child can feel safe to reconnect.

Reminder: connection doesn't always need words. Sometimes love and safety are felt most deeply through calm, presence, and patience.

1. Prepare a cozy spot: a blanket, some soft lighting, maybe a favorite stuffed animal or pillow.

2. Start with silence: Sit together quietly, no talking needed. Breathe slowly and let them sense your calm.

3. Offer connection without words: Draw together, build with blocks, or trace shapes in sand or playdough - something peaceful and steady.

4. Add gentle communication: After a few minutes, invite your child to share if they want ~ a color that shows how they feel, a drawing, or just one word that matches what's in their heart.

5. End with reassurance: *"No matter how quiet things get, I'm always here. You can take your time."*

Keep going ~ you are shaping their world with care.

PART III:

FAMILY DYNAMICS AND RELATIONSHIPS

BUILDING A STRONG BOND WITH YOUR CHILD

Building Connection: Finding Your Shared Space

Have you ever looked at your child and felt, *Wow, this is my own flesh and blood* ~ yet somehow sensed a distance between you? Parenting is one of life's greatest joys, but it's also complex. Every child arrives with their own personality, their own way of communicating, and their own emotional needs. Sometimes closeness doesn't come as easily ~ or as quickly ~ as we hope.

It can feel frustrating or even disheartening when connection doesn't happen naturally. The truth is, connection rarely appears on its own. It grows through intention, patience, and a willingness to step into your child's world. It's found in shared spaces ~ moments of play, laughter, conversation, or even quiet time together. These small, everyday experiences become bridges that help you understand your child more deeply and help them feel seen, safe, and understood.

Instant bonds are rare. Connection isn't about perfection; it's about presence. What resonates with one child may not resonate with another. Part of parenting is learning to meet your child where they are ~ emotionally and mentally ~ instead of waiting for them to step into your world. And this often means exploring the things *they* love, not just the things you naturally enjoy.

Some children respond to words; others feel closeness through actions or shared experiences. Some feel loved through physical closeness ~ a hug, a cuddle, a gentle touch ~ while others feel it through thoughtful gestures or a small gift made especially for them.

Yet no matter how your child connects, one truth holds steady: you need to enter their world alongside them. You may not be naturally interested in the things they adore ~ their games, hobbies, shows, collections ~ but your curiosity speaks love. Saying *"Show me,"* or *"Teach me,"* opens the door to closeness.

This is where we can take a moment to look inward and see how we might be meeting them halfway. It helps to pause and reflect on the choices we make as parents. How often do we plan outings or activities based on what we enjoy? Maybe we choose the restaurant we like, or the movie we want to see, or the store we prefer to browse. We might plan a weekend around things that feel fun or relaxing to us ~ without fully realizing our child is simply tagging along. None of this is wrong. It's just easy to forget that children don't always feel connected when they're following us through our world.

So take a moment and ask yourself:

When was the last time I asked my child what they wanted to do? ***Where they wanted*** *to go? What **they were** curious about?*

These questions matter, because they shift the center of gravity. They tell your child, *You matter. Your interests matter. I want to know what lights you up.*

You can even try small, simple experiments:

- Let them choose the place for your next outing ~ even if it's somewhere you wouldn't pick.
- Say yes when they ask you to watch a show they love or play a game with them.
- Invite them to teach you something they're good at, even if you feel awkward or out of place.

These moments are powerful. They communicate, *I want to understand your world, not pull you into mine.* Exploring their world sometimes leads you to discoveries of your own ~ small joys that grow into a shared space, something belonging to both of you.

Children feel deeply valued when we make room for what matters to them. That simple shift ~ stepping into their interests with curiosity ~ often becomes the very place where trust, closeness, and connection truly begin.

Often, the most meaningful bonds form in the simplest moments: a shared laugh, reading side by side, or creating something with your hands. These quiet moments communicate, I see you. I value you. I want to know who you are. That message becomes the foundation for trust, love, and a sacred, lasting connection.

Personal Reflection ~ Huge Tip!

I discovered that one of the most powerful ways to build a lasting bond is to nurture something together. It doesn't have to be big ~ a shared project, hobby, or responsibility creates moments of teamwork, empathy, and mutual reliance.

For me, **raising a pet with my child** has been transformative. Caring for a living creature together brings shared purpose, daily commitment, and opportunities for gentle communication. It's a small universe of responsibility where love, patience, and connection grow naturally.

For me, raising a pet with my child has been transformative. Caring for a living creature together brings shared purpose, daily commitment, and opportunities for gentle communication. It's a small world of responsibility where love, patience, and connection grow naturally. Working as a team teaches accountability ~ you learn to rely on one another and to care for something you both love. There's a quiet joy in knowing that if one of you is busy, the other will step in. Over time, those small acts of care build trust and deepen your bond.

That same sense of connection can grow in other ways too ~ tending a garden, joining a sport, or building something side by side. It's about growing together, nurturing something that matters, and sharing the experience of watching it take shape. These moments become the kind children carry with them for life ~ reminders of love built through something you created, cared for, and enjoyed together.

The key isn't the activity itself ~ it's showing up, consistently, side by side. It's the intention to be present, to notice, and to nurture a connection rooted in mutual joy. When you make space for these shared moments, you give your child something invaluable: the certainty that they are seen, valued, and loved.

LOVE YOUR SIBLINGS ~ DON'T TAKE THEM FOR GRANTED

The Unique Bond Between Siblings

Have you ever thought about what your own relationship with a sibling taught you? Maybe it was closeness and laughter. Maybe it was distance or unspoken tension. Some people grow up never fully forgiving their sibling, while others find new understanding later in life. Whatever your story, it shapes how you see the bond between your own children and how you guide them through it.

Our children often don't realize, especially when they're young, that the bond between siblings is unlike any other. It grows from shared experiences, childhood memories, and a closeness that can last a lifetime. While friendships may come and go, siblings can remain a constant source of love, support, and understanding.

It's easy for children to take this bond for granted, assuming their sibling will always be around. As parents, we can gently encourage them to cherish one another while they can. Help your child see their sibling as someone who truly knows them. Siblings often witness each other's hardest moments, celebrate each other's wins, and walk side by side through life's milestones. Even when teasing or disagreements happen, the love beneath those moments is irreplaceable.

Sibling relationships aren't always smooth. Rivalry, jealousy, and competition are normal. Many conflicts come from feeling left out, overlooked, or less important. Often, a child who lashes out is reflecting their own pain, wanting the other sibling to feel what they are struggling to express. Pausing to notice the feelings behind the behavior, instead of rushing to discipline, opens the door to empathy and understanding.

I know this personally. Growing up, I wasn't always the nicest to my little sister. I carried my own struggles and jealousy and sometimes took them out on her. At the same time, I looked out for her and protected her while I felt I had no one to protect me. Those contradictions shaped our relationship ~ love and frustration intertwined. When we both became mothers, we found a new connection ~ a common ground that brought us close again. Later, when she was diagnosed with breast cancer and passed away, I wished I could go back, express more care, or soften my jealousy. She was one hundred percent blood ~ no one can replace that bond. That experience shapes how I guide my children in valuing and protecting their sibling relationships.

When each child feels seen, valued, and reassured of their place in the family, the need to compete or tear others down often fades. A home built on love, fairness, and respect helps siblings grow from rivalry into lifelong allies ~ supportive, protective, and proud of each other's uniqueness. Reflecting on our own experiences with siblings can help us guide our children in noticing each other's perspectives, appreciating differences, and understanding the feelings behind conflicts. In this way, they begin to see the world through one another's eyes, deepening connection and empathy in ways that words alone cannot capture.

Activity:

Switch Lives for a Day

This playful exercise helps siblings step into each other's shoes and build empathy.

Steps:

1. Assign each sibling the role of the other.

They'll act, speak, and take on responsibilities as their brother or sister would. This could include chores, hobbies, or even wearing each other's clothes. The goal isn't to impersonate but to experience life from a new perspective.

2. Guide the activity with questions:

- *"What's your favorite food?"*
- *"What music makes you happy?"*
- *"What frustrates you?"*
- They answer as they believe their sibling would.

3. At the end of the day, gather as a family to reflect:

- *What surprised you?*
- *What was difficult or eye-opening?*
- *What do you now appreciate more about your sibling?*

This reflection helps children see life through each other's lens, creating empathy and strengthening emotional connection.

Food For Thought

After the activity, take a quiet moment to reflect on your own experiences with siblings:

- *Were there times of jealousy, rivalry, or misunderstanding in your childhood?*
- *Did you sometimes take your sibling for granted or act out from your own pain?*
- *Are there moments you wish you could revisit, or words you wish you had said?*

Now, think about your children:

- *How can you help them build empathy, celebrate each other's uniqueness, and forgive quickly?*
- *What did you learn from your relationship with your sibling that you want to pass on to your children?*

By reflecting on our own story, we teach through example honesty, growth, and emotional awareness. We show our children that it's never too late to learn, heal, and strengthen the bonds that truly matter.

DIVORCE

Helping Your Child Navigate Divorce: Healing Together

Have you noticed how children often carry feelings they don't yet have words for? Divorce shakes a family in ways bigger than we sometimes realize. Confusion, sadness, fear, or guilt can show up differently depending on a child's age. Some may act out, others may withdraw quietly, and many simply try to make sense of emotions they don't fully understand. Even a quick separation can be challenging, but preparing ahead can make a huge difference.

One of the most important things we can do is acknowledge what our children are feeling. Show them ~ again and again ~ that their emotions are real, that loving both parents is safe, and that they will continue to be supported no matter what changes. Our children notice how we handle change just as much as what we say. Our anger, grief, fear, or sadness will surface. How we respond becomes the lesson, far more than any words. Slowing down, naming our feelings, and showing that emotions can be managed with care teaches them how to do the same.

Preparation helps protect everyone's emotional safety. Thinking through what will be said, who can support your child, and who can support you in the conversation sets the stage for stability. Planning even a day ahead ~ reviewing what might happen and how to respond ~ ensures that you are mindful and present, instead of reacting in the moment. The whole family needs support. Doing it in silence, without help, doesn't prepare anyone for the emotions that will surface.

Children need space to share, without judgment, interruption, or quick fixes. Open questions can help guide them:

- *"How are you feeling today?"*
- *"What's been the hardest part for you lately?"*
- *"What could help you feel safer or more supported right now?"*

Pay close attention to how your child communicates without words. Silence, mood swings, withdrawal, or acting out aren't signs that everything is okay. They are communication ~ a signal that understanding, guidance, and reassurance are needed. Children who seem "resilient" are often just surviving, carrying emotions that haven't yet been named or processed. Real resilience grows when they are seen, supported, and guided through their pain, not left to manage it alone.

Children don't stop feeling just because they appear fine. They go to school, do homework, smile when expected, all while carrying emotions that need attention. Trying to replace what they need with a movie, toy, treat, or activity may feel easier in the moment, but it doesn't give them the security, understanding, and connection they truly need.

Parents also need support. Being mindful of your own struggles ~ and seeking support from a trusted friend, counselor, or community ~ helps you stay grounded and present for your child. Making sure you have someone to lean on ensures your child doesn't feel responsible for carrying your emotions. Leaning on children to manage your emotions is unfair and can add to their burden. Your child is likely struggling more than you realize. Being calm, attentive, and present is the most powerful support you can give.

Encourage your children to ask questions, express doubts, and share fears. Keeping things from them to protect them can backfire, leaving them feeling abandoned or in the dark. True protection comes from creating a safe space to process the truth together, allowing them to face change with support rather than alone.

Take a quiet moment and think about how you're showing up for your child right now. *Are you really giving them space to share what's going on inside? Have you prepared yourself so that both of you have support in place for the tough conversations that might come?* Notice if you're leaning on your child in ways that add to their emotional load. *Who can you turn to for support so you can be fully present, calm, and steady for them?*

Even when everything feels uncertain, you have the power to create a space where your child feels safe, seen, and loved. With your patience, attention, and care, they can learn that their feelings matter, that it's okay to struggle, and that being honest about emotions doesn't make them weak ~ it makes them human. You don't have to fix everything. Just showing up, listening, and being there consistently is the strongest thing you can do.

Helping our children navigate a divorce isn't about fixing everything for them or shielding them from hard truths. It's about giving them space to notice what they feel, to name it, and to practice expressing it in ways that feel safe. Staying present, patient, and consistent allows them to understand that their emotions are real, that asking questions is okay, and that even in the middle of change, they are deeply loved and supported.

Quiet moments of reflection, drawing, journaling, or simply talking together help children recognize and process what's happening inside them. By creating these gentle opportunities, we guide them in understanding themselves, trusting the adults around them, and finding small ways to express and release the feelings that might otherwise remain unspoken.

Activities:

Helping Children Process Their Emotions

1. Feelings Journals

Give your child a notebook or journal where they can write or draw how they're feeling. Younger children, or kids who find words hard, can use drawing instead. Encourage them to show both happy and hard moments. Have them share only if they want to, and remind them you're there to listen without judging. This helps them understand their feelings and know they have a safe adult to turn to.

2. Emotion Stones

Collect a few smooth stones and paint simple symbols for different emotions on each: happy, sad, angry, scared, confused, or worried. Each day, or whenever strong feelings arise, let your child pick a stone that matches their mood. Use it as a conversation starter:

- *"I see you chose the sad stone today. Can you tell me a little about why you're feeling sad?"*
- *"What could make you feel a little lighter or safer right now?"*

These stones let children show how they feel in a way that's easy and safe, and it helps start gentle conversations about their emotions.

Food for Thought ~ Healing Together

Divorce is hard for children ~ and it's hard for us, too. Our own feelings of loss, frustration, or fear often mirror theirs. When we notice our child's reactions stirring something inside us, it's an opportunity to pause, reflect, and grow alongside them.

Ask yourself:

- *What in this moment is triggering me, and why?*
- *How can I respond with calm and understanding even when I feel emotional?*
- *How can I show that it's okay to feel deeply, struggle, and still move forward with love?*

By exploring our own triggers as we support our children, we teach a powerful lesson: **it's okay to feel, it's okay to struggle, and it's possible to heal together.**

A NEW BABY BRINGS BIG CHANGES FOR EVERYONE.

NEW BABY

Welcoming a New Baby: Helping Older Children Feel Loved and Included

Bringing a new baby home is an exciting time, but it can also stir up a lot of emotions ~ for you, for your older child, and for the family as a whole. I remember when my second child arrived. I felt a wave of guilt and worry for my firstborn, like somehow dividing my love was a betrayal. Those first days were emotional; there were even tears. Over time, a new rhythm formed, and our family found its balance. It's important to remember that this transition isn't just about your older child's feelings ~ you, too, are working through big emotions. Give yourself permission to feel them, and don't hesitate to reach out for support. When you take care of yourself, you can be fully present for both of your children.

Helping your older child feel involved and valued is key. Let them know they are still deeply loved, that they remain an essential part of the family, and that their new role as an older sibling is special. Spend intentional time with them, listen to their thoughts and worries, and invite them to participate in caring for the baby in age-appropriate ways. Even small tasks ~ handing you a clean diaper, stroking the baby's head gently, or singing softly together ~ help them feel important and connected.

Before the baby even arrives, consider giving your older child a baby doll to "care for." This allows them to mimic your actions and practice nurturing on their own level, which can help ease anxiety and build excitement. Talk with them about the baby growing in your belly, let them help prepare, and encourage them to imagine what it will be like to have a new sibling.

Once the baby is home, continue to include your older child in small caregiving tasks and make sure to carve out one-on-one time just for them. Read a book together while the baby naps, play a quick game, or enjoy a quiet snack. These moments remind them that they are seen and valued, even among the demands of caring for a newborn. Be open and honest about why the baby might need extra attention at times, and invite your older child to help when they can. Seeing this as a family effort, rather than a parent-only responsibility, strengthens bonds and reduces feelings of jealousy.

It's natural for older children to experience a mix of excitement, curiosity, and even jealousy. Acknowledging all of their feelings without judgment helps them feel safe and understood. When children feel secure in their place within the family, they are more likely to embrace their new role as a sibling with confidence and joy.

Activities:

Helping Your Older Child Adjust to a New Baby

Welcoming a new baby is full of joy, but it can also stir big feelings for your older child - jealousy, worry, or feeling left out. You can help them feel included and loved by giving them meaningful ways to be part of caring for the baby.

1. Special Job Chart: Give your older child small, age-appropriate tasks to "help" with the baby. Examples:

- Bring a clean diaper or wipes
- Sing or talk softly to the baby
- Help pick out the baby's outfit for the day
- Fetch a pacifier or soft blanket
- Hand you a water bottle or burp cloth during feeding

2. Story Time Together: Invite your older child to "read" aloud to the baby or help turn pages while you're nearby. These moments like this create connection and give them a chance to share in the baby's world.

3. Family Check-In: At the end of the day, gently ask:

- *What did you enjoy helping with today?*
- *How do you think the baby is adjusting?*
- *Are there ways we can all support each other as a family?*

4. One-on-One Time: Make a short, special moment each day just for your older child - a cuddle, a quick game, or sharing a snack. These times remind them that they are still a unique, loved part of the family and that your attention isn't divided.

By including your older child in the process and intentionally nurturing your bond, you help them feel seen, capable, and loved. They learn that caring for the baby is a shared family effort, and they gain a sense of connection and pride in their new role. With patience, intention, and a little creativity, the arrival of a new baby can become a joyful and unifying experience for the whole family.

Food for Thought ~ Caring for Yourself While Caring for Everyone Else

Welcoming a new baby doesn't just shift your older child's world ~ it shifts yours, too. Sleep deprivation, endless feedings, and the constant tug of attention can leave you feeling stretched thin, guilty, or even a little resentful at times. It's okay to admit that. Parenting a newborn while nurturing an older child is one of life's toughest balancing acts.

Remember: your feelings matter. When you acknowledge your own emotions ~ whether it's exhaustion, anxiety, or sadness ~ you show your children that it's normal to feel deeply and that taking care of yourself is important. The more you give yourself permission to pause, breathe, and reflect, the more present and patient you can be with both of your children.

Try to notice your triggers, the moments when you feel frustrated or overwhelmed. Sometimes, these moments reveal unmet needs or fatigue that you've been ignoring. Reflecting on what stirs up those feelings can help you respond more calmly and intentionally, rather than reacting out of stress or guilt.

Here's the powerful part: by observing your own feelings and showing healthy ways to cope with them, you're teaching your older child an invaluable lesson in emotional awareness. They learn that it's okay to have big feelings, that everyone makes mistakes, and that taking a moment to pause, reflect, and respond thoughtfully is a sign of strength, not weakness.

You are learning and growing alongside them. Some days will be messy, emotional, and exhausting; and that's okay. This journey of adjustment is not just about helping your children thrive; it's also about finding your footing as a parent in a family that has grown in ways you didn't imagine.

RELATIONSHIPS

Teaching Children About Relationships: Learning Together

Our children don't just learn about relationships from what we tell them ~ they learn from what they see. Every day, they're watching how we love, how we argue, how we set boundaries, and how we treat the people around us ~ including ourselves. We are their first example of what love and respect look like.

The way we show up in our relationships matters deeply. The way we talk to our partner, the way we handle conflict, the way we care for our own hearts ~ it all teaches them something. What they experience with us becomes their blueprint for how love should feel. If they see us accepting mistreatment, struggling to say no, or staying quiet when something doesn't feel right, they might grow up thinking that's just what love looks like.

Relationships teach our children more than anything we could tell them. Every hug, every argument, every moment of honesty shows them what love feels like, what respect looks like, and how to treat others ~ and themselves. Losing people they care about is painful, but it can also teach them how to bounce back and how to hold love in their hearts even when it changes or ends. When we notice our own mistakes, reflect on why we acted a certain way, and make amends when we can, we show our children that relationships matter, that they are worth caring for, and that every connection ~ even the messy or hard ones ~ carries lessons that help us grow. This also helps them understand that sometimes walking away from someone who isn't healthy for them doesn't mean they've failed; it means they are strong enough to protect their own heart.

Relationships aren't always simple. We can gently show our children that connections can be messy, beautiful, confusing, and sometimes don't last forever. Encourage them to notice the lessons each relationship brings. Some lessons are joyful and light, while others quietly open their hearts and help them see love in a new way.

Parenting has been one of my greatest mirrors. It has shown me the parts of myself I didn't want to see ~ the patterns I repeated, the triggers I carried, and the ways I've had to grow. I've learned to pause before reacting, to see situations through my children's eyes, and to understand that we are all learning together.

I often think about my sister. Growing up, I wasn't always kind to her. I carried my own pain, jealousy, and confusion, and too often she got caught in it. I also protected her fiercely ~ because deep down, I knew what it felt like to have no one on my side. Years later, when she became sick with breast cancer and passed away, I wished I could have done so many things differently. Losing her taught me the weight of love left unspoken. That loss changed me. It taught me about forgiveness, presence, and the importance of showing love while we still can.

That experience reshaped how I parent. It reminds me that relationships are sacred, fragile, and worth honoring ~ but never at the cost of yourself. I carry that lesson forward with my children, gently teaching them that real love is honest, kind, and safe. It shows them that boundaries are necessary, that love should make room for who they truly are, and that every connection, whether joyful or challenging, is a chance to grow, forgive, and learn.

When People Are Taken Away

Sometimes, people who matter deeply to our children can be taken from their lives suddenly, leaving a hole that feels confusing and painful. It might be a family member who grows distant, a mentor who disappears, or an adult they trusted who is no longer allowed to spend time with them. Children may not understand why the change happened, and without clear communication, it can feel like a personal rejection. They may wonder if they did something wrong, or if they somehow weren't deserving of love. These experiences can leave children feeling alone, hurt, and unsure whether they can trust the adults around them.

I know this feeling intimately. When I was a child, a woman came into my life who gave me something I was missing at home ~ care, attention, and connection. She filled a space I didn't even know could be filled. Suddenly, without explanation, she was gone. I didn't understand why. I blocked the pain for years, but inside, I carried confusion, sadness, and anger. I wondered if it was my fault, or if someone else had been jealous of our bond. For a long time, I couldn't talk about it, and the hurt shaped the way I felt about myself, trust, and love. Looking back now, I can see how that loss, as painful as it was, set me on a journey to discover my worth, my purpose, and the ability to trust and love myself even when people leave.

Friendships can disappear, sometimes without warning. A best friend might move away, a fight could happen, or family issues might create distance. Children can feel abandoned, upset, or angry. These experiences often leave them looking for ways to fill the gap. They might act out, pull away, or try to control other parts of their life to feel safer. Losing friends is hard, but it also teaches children that they can bounce back, care for themselves, and appreciate the people who treat them well, even when some relationships end.

When children lose someone they care about ~ a friend, a mentor, or even someone we, as parents, might have taken out of their lives ~ it can shake them deeply. They may feel hurt, angry, confused, or abandoned, and sometimes they may even direct some of that anger toward us. It's tempting to try to fix the feelings or make the pain go away, but what they really need most is our presence. Letting them feel their emotions without judgment, just being there beside them, can quietly mean more than anything we could say. Checking in with simple questions like, *"Are you hurting right now?"* or *"How can I be here for you?"* shows them we notice, we care, and they aren't alone.

If loss isn't processed with understanding and support, the impact can stretch far into adulthood. Children may develop coping habits to manage the pain themselves ~ withdrawing, overachieving, trying to control situations, or even turning to unhealthy habits. When we show up for them, listen, and let them express their feelings safely, we help stop these patterns from taking hold. Being present, patient, and loving while letting them work through their emotions teaches them that feelings are safe, that love doesn't disappear when people leave, and that stepping away ~ or coping with the loss ~ of any relationship isn't failure but part of learning and growing. Simply holding space for them ~ without trying to fix, explain, or erase the pain ~ gives them something lasting: the quiet understanding that they are seen, loved, and not alone.

Reflecting on Our Own Actions

As parents, we need to be honest with ourselves. *Have we ever taken someone away from our child out of jealousy, insecurity, or fear? Have we let our own emotions get in the way of their happiness?*

If we notice this in ourselves, it's important to reflect. *Why do we feel intimidated? Is it low self-esteem? How can we strengthen our relationship with our child so we feel connected, rather than jealous?* Sometimes, we might even have the chance, in the future, to have an honest conversation with our child about the past. Sharing our vulnerability, apologizing for any hurt caused, and showing our feelings can help rebuild trust and understanding.

Relationships teach our children more than anything we could ever tell them. Every hug, every argument, every moment of honesty shows them what love feels like, what respect looks like, and how to treat others ~ and themselves. Losing people they care about is painful, but it can also teach them how to recover and how to hold love in their hearts even when connections change or end. When we notice our own mistakes, reflect on why we acted a certain way, and make amends when we can, we show our children that relationships matter and that they are worth caring for. Every connection ~ even the messy or hard ones ~ offers lessons that help them grow. Practicing these lessons together, exploring how to respond, set boundaries, and understand emotions, helps children build the skills to navigate relationships with confidence, care, and honesty.

Activities:

Relationship Skills

1. Respectful Responses

This activity helps children express boundaries calmly and confidently. Role-play situations such as:

- A friend making a rude comment
- Someone pressuring them to do something uncomfortable
- A sibling or classmate invading their personal space

Coach them to respond with statements like:

- "I don't like when you talk to me that way."
- "I need you to respect my decision."
- "That doesn't feel right to me, and I'm choosing not to do it."

These phrases build assertiveness and teach that it's possible to be firm without being unkind.

2. What Would You Say?

Give your child scenarios involving friends, family, or, for older kids, romantic relationships. Ask: *"What would you say or do here?"* Examples:

- Your friend keeps canceling plans last minute.
- A classmate is spreading rumors about you.
- Someone pressures you to ignore your boundaries.

Talk through their responses together. Offer gentle feedback and explore healthier alternatives. These discussions build confidence and emotional clarity.

3. Reflect on Real-Life Lessons

Encourage your child to think about times when relationships felt hard, unfair, or even painful. Discuss:

- What they learned about themselves
- How they could respond differently next time
- How to handle mixed emotions like love, frustration, and disappointment

4. Mapping My Relationships

This activity helps children reflect on the people in their lives, understand how each relationship makes them feel, and learn that relationships can be messy, beautiful, and full of lessons.

What You'll Need:

- Large sheet of paper or notebook

- Colored pencils, markers, or crayons
- Stickers (optional)

Steps:

1. Draw Yourself in the Center: Draw a circle in the middle of the page with your child's name inside. This represents them - the starting point of all connections.

2. Add People Around You: Around the circle, have your child draw or write the names of family members, friends, teachers, or anyone important in their life.

3. Show Connections: Draw lines connecting the central circle (your child) to each person. Use different colors or styles of lines to show how each relationship feels:

- Solid line = strong, safe connection
- Dotted line = needs more attention
- Zigzag line = sometimes challenging or confusing

4. Label the Feelings: Beside each line, write a word, phrase, or draw a small emoji that represents how the relationship makes them feel: happy, safe, loved, frustrated, confused, excited, etc.

5. Reflect Together: Ask gentle, open-ended questions:

- *"Which relationships feel the safest to you?"*
- *"Are there people you feel unsure about sometimes?"*
- *"What can you do to help make a tricky relationship feel better?"*
- *"How do you think you help others feel safe and loved?"*

6. Optional Creative Touch: Let your child decorate the page with symbols, colors, or stickers to show fun moments, shared experiences, or love and support in each relationship.

By exploring these activities, children learn to express themselves, respect boundaries, and understand that connections can be messy, beautiful, and full of growth. They gain confidence, empathy, and the tools to navigate life's relationships with courage and heart.

I like these activities because they encourage children to see relationships as living, dynamic, and full of lessons. It shows them that:

- It's normal for some relationships to feel messy or challenging.
- Healthy relationships are built on respect, care, and honesty.
- They have the power to contribute to positive connections.
- Every relationship ~ easy or hard ~ teaches us something about ourselves and others.

It also gives you, as a parent, insight into how your child experiences connections, where they feel safe, and where they may need support or guidance.

PART IV:
CLOSING

YOU CAN DO THIS!!! ~ I AM IN THIS WITH YOU!!!

You Can Do This

Parenting is one of the hardest things we'll ever do.
It is also one of the most beautiful.
There is no manual.
No perfect formula.
Only our best intentions.

Our lived experiences.
The lessons we carry from our own childhoods.

I am learning. I am enough. I am present.

So much of how we parent comes from what shaped us:
what we needed but didn't receive,
what hurt us,
what healed us,
and what we promised ourselves we would one day do differently.

Healing our own childhood wounds is one of the most powerful ways
to show up differently for our children.
It's not easy.
Looking back rarely is.
But it's how we stop repeating what hurt us and start building something new.

I am breaking cycles. I am creating love. I am changing the story.

When we respond with empathy instead of reaction,
patience instead of frustration,
we're not just parenting ~ we're rewriting a legacy.

Our children need guidance.
They also need gentleness.
They need to know they are loved for *who they are*, not *what they achieve*.
They need to feel safe to make mistakes.
To cry.
To be imperfect ~ just as we do.

I am kind. I am gentle. I am steady.

When we make space for their full humanity,
we remind them ~ and ourselves ~ that love doesn't have to be earned.

It's already theirs.

I am enough. My child is enough. We are enough.

───

A Message From My Heart

I didn't write this book as an expert.
I wrote it as a mother.
One who has stumbled.
Fallen.
Learned through experience.

I am not here to judge.
Not here to criticize.
I am here to connect.
To inspire.
To remind you ~ you are not alone.

There were times in my life when I didn't feel seen, heard, or understood.
Both as a child.
And later, as a parent trying to do better with what I knew.

Those experiences shaped me.
They also broke me open.
They taught me how deeply early wounds can linger.
How easily they can resurface in the way we love, speak, or react to our children.

Many of us carry childhood stories that still whisper:
You're not enough.
You have to be perfect.
Don't speak up.

Our parents didn't mean to plant those seeds.
They were doing the best they could with what they knew.

When we don't heal, those messages quietly pass down through
generations.

This book is my way of saying: it stops here.
We can break those cycles.
We can learn a new way.
A way built on awareness.
Compassion.
Healing.

*I am breaking old patterns. I am creating something new. I am doing my
best.*

And through it all, one truth has become clear:
We do not have to do this alone.

We Are In This Together

I am still learning.
Every single day.
I catch myself reacting from old patterns.
I say words I wish I could take back.

Every day gives us another chance to pause.
To repair.
To grow.

There is no perfect parent.
There are only honest ones.
Those willing to learn.
To apologize.

To keep trying.

I am patient. I am honest. I am present.

Healing often begins in the moments we think we've failed.
When we soften.
When we listen.
When we choose connection over control.

That's when everything begins to shift.

As parents, we are the bridge between what was...
...and what can be.

We carry both.
The pain of the past.
The possibility of something better.

When we respond with empathy instead of anger.
Listen instead of dismiss.
Love instead of shame.

We create a new story.
One our children will carry forward long after us.

I am love. I am change. I am hope.

Let's promise to keep showing up.
Imperfectly.
Wholeheartedly.
Together.

We may not have all the answers.
But we have love.
And that is more than enough.

"We may not be perfect, but we are present, learning, and loving ~ and that is more than enough."

─

Parenting Affirmations:
Daily Reminders for Your Heart

I am doing my best, and that is enough.
I am patient, even when it's hard.
I am present, even when life feels busy.
I show love through action, words, and heart.
I am learning and growing, just like my child.
I trust my child to explore, stumble, and rise.
I listen before I react.
I choose connection over control.
I honor both my child's needs and my own.
I show strength, courage, self-love, and authenticity.
I celebrate mistakes as opportunities to grow.
I forgive myself, and I forgive my child.
I am a bridge between the past and a better future.
I am love, I am hope, I am enough.

Repeat these daily, out loud or silently, and let each one remind you that you are the kind of parent your child needs most: steady, loving, and fully human.

REFLECTION AND LOOKING AHEAD

Dear Parent,

Congratulations on making it through *Bloom*. You took the time to notice, reflect, and plant seeds of awareness for yourself and your child. Thank you for showing up, for reading with an open heart, and for choosing growth. Every page you finished, every moment you paused, and every insight you gained are the roots of lasting change.

Flourish is the next step on this journey. The seeds you planted in *Bloom* are ready to grow. This book will guide you in nurturing them ~ in exploring your own patterns, understanding your triggers, and seeing the old stories that have shaped your choices. It is not about perfection. It is about noticing, reflecting, and responding with intention.

Parenting while healing is challenging, yet powerful. Every pause before a reaction, every moment you respond thoughtfully instead of automatically, is an act of love. Every time you choose connection over habit, you strengthen the bond with your child while also caring for yourself.

You are not alone. You are learning, your child is learning, and together you are growing. The roots you tend today will support a more present, compassionate, and emotionally safe environment for your child ~ and for yourself.

Bloom showed you how to see. *Flourish* shows you how to grow. May these pages give you both clarity and courage, guidance and grace, as you continue planting, tending, and nurturing the life and relationship you desire.

Keep practicing.

Keep reflecting.
Keep choosing connection.
Keep choosing love.

I am proud of the work you are doing and honored to walk
beside you as you continue this journey.

With love and gratitude,

Heather

THE PATH FORWARD

From *Bloom* to *Flourish*

As we close this book, I want to remind you of something simple but powerful: awareness is the beginning of change. Every chapter you've read, every moment that made you pause, and every truth that stirred something in you ~ these are seeds. You planted them by choosing to grow, to reflect, and to show up differently for your child and for yourself.

This is only the foundation.

Flourish will take those seeds and help them grow into something extraordinary. This next book is about action, practice, and transformation. It will guide you through the patterns we carry, the generational wounds that shape our choices, and the ways we can heal ourselves so we can respond to our children with clarity, compassion, and love. The change you experience as a parent will ripple outward, affecting every interaction, every conversation, and every moment of connection with your child.

Everything you learned in *Bloom* ~ noticing, reflecting, pausing, understanding ~ now becomes the tools to communicate, guide, and nurture in ways that can reverse patterns, repair wounds, and create a safe, emotionally rich environment for your child.

Your healing directly supports your child's growth. The awareness you've gained allows you to respond with presence instead of reaction, to lead with empathy, and to model emotional strength. This isn't about being perfect; it's about becoming the parent your child needs and the person you aspire to be.

If *Bloom* opened your eyes to new ways of seeing your child and yourself, *Flourish* will show you how to live those lessons every day. You will learn to recognize your triggers, understand your reactions, and gently rewrite the story you may have carried for years. Your child will feel the difference ~ calmer, safer, and more seen. Your relationship can deepen in ways you may not have imagined.

Thank you for walking through these pages with an open heart. You and your child deserve a home built on trust, love, and understanding ~ and you are already creating it.

When you're ready, let's continue this journey together in *Flourish*. Your next chapter awaits, and the transformation is truly remarkable.

This is not the end ~ it's the next beginning.
Carry what you've learned gently,
let it take root in daily moments,
and trust that growth continues long after the pages close.
Because every bloom whispers the promise of flourishing.

www.ingramcontent.com/pod-product-compliance
Lightning Source LLC
Chambersburg PA
CBHW040853120626
46551CB00001B/4